CLARENCE
THOMAS

CLARENCE THOMAS

Norman L. Macht

CHELSEA HOUSE PUBLISHERS
New York   Philadelphia

The author is indebted to Leola Williams, Ricky Silberman, Cliff Faddis, Freddie Framble, the good people at the Savannah Catholic Diocese office, Supreme Court Public Information Officer Toni House, and especially Justice Thomas, for helping me get this story right.

Chelsea House Publishers
Editorial Director Richard Rennert
Executive Managing Editor Karyn Gullen Browne
Copy Chief Robin James
Picture Editor Adrian G. Allen
Creative Director Robert Mitchell
Art Director Joan Ferrigno
Production Manager Sallye Scott

Black Americans of Achievement
Senior Editor Philip Koslow

Staff for CLARENCE THOMAS
Editorial Assistant Sydra Mallery
Senior Designer Marjorie Zaum
Picture Researcher Matthew Dudley
Cover Illustrator Kye Carbone

First Printing

1 3 5 7 9 8 6 4 2

Library of Congress Cataloging-in-Publication Data
Macht, Norman L. (Norman Lee), 1929–
    Clarence Thomas/Norman L. Macht.
        p. cm. — (Black Americans of achievement)
    Includes bibliographical references and index.
        ISBN 0-7910-1883-0.
               0-7910-1912-8 (pbk.)
    1. Thomas, Clarence, 1948– —Juvenile Literature. 2.
Judges—United States—Biography—Juvenile literature. [1.Thomas,
Clarence, 1948– . 2. Judges. 3. United States. Supreme
Court—Biography. 4. Afro-Americans—Biography.] I. Title. II. Series.
347.73'2634—dc20   94-44353
[B]   CIP
[347.3073534]   AC
[B]

Frontispiece: Clarence Thomas walks in front of the U.S. Supreme Court building on November 1, 1991, shortly after becoming the 106th justice in the Court's history.

CONTENTS

BLACK AMERICANS OF ACHIEVEMENT

HENRY AARON
baseball great

KAREEM ABDUL-JABBAR
basketball great

RALPH ABERNATHY
civil rights leader

ALVIN AILEY
choreographer

MUHAMMAD ALI
heavyweight champion

RICHARD ALLEN
*religious leader and
social activist*

MAYA ANGELOU
author

LOUIS ARMSTRONG
musician

ARTHUR ASHE
tennis great

JOSEPHINE BAKER
entertainer

JAMES BALDWIN
author

BENJAMIN BANNEKER
scientist and mathematician

AMIRI BARAKA
poet and playwright

COUNT BASIE
bandleader and composer

ROMARE BEARDEN
artist

JAMES BECKWOURTH
frontiersman

MARY MCLEOD BETHUNE
educator

JULIAN BOND
civil rights leader and politician

GWENDOLYN BROOKS
poet

JIM BROWN
football great

STOKELY CARMICHAEL
civil rights leader

GEORGE WASHINGTON
CARVER
botanist

RAY CHARLES
musician

CHARLES CHESNUTT
author

JOHN COLTRANE
musician

BILL COSBY
entertainer

PAUL CUFFE
merchant and abolitionist

COUNTEE CULLEN
poet

BENJAMIN DAVIS, SR., AND
BENJAMIN DAVIS, JR.
military leaders

MILES DAVIS
musician

SAMMY DAVIS, JR.
entertainer

FATHER DIVINE
religious leader

FREDERICK DOUGLASS
abolitionist editor

CHARLES DREW
physician

W. E. B. DU BOIS
scholar and activist

PAUL LAURENCE DUNBAR
poet

KATHERINE DUNHAM
dancer and choreographer

DUKE ELLINGTON
bandleader and composer

RALPH ELLISON
author

JULIUS ERVING
basketball great

JAMES FARMER
civil rights leader

ELLA FITZGERALD
singer

MARCUS GARVEY
black nationalist leader

JOSH GIBSON
baseball great

DIZZY GILLESPIE
musician

WHOOPI GOLDBERG
entertainer

ALEX HALEY
author

PRINCE HALL
social reformer

MATTHEW HENSON
explorer

CHESTER HIMES
author

BILLIE HOLIDAY
singer

LENA HORNE
entertainer

LANGSTON HUGHES
poet

ZORA NEALE HURSTON
author

JESSE JACKSON
civil rights leader and politician

MICHAEL JACKSON
entertainer

JACK JOHNSON
heavyweight champion

JAMES WELDON JOHNSON
author

MAGIC JOHNSON
basketball great

SCOTT JOPLIN
composer

BARBARA JORDAN
politician

MICHAEL JORDAN
basketball great

CORETTA SCOTT KING
civil rights leader

MARTIN LUTHER KING, JR.
civil rights leader

LEWIS LATIMER
scientist

SPIKE LEE
filmmaker

CARL LEWIS
champion athlete

JOE LOUIS
heavyweight champion

RONALD MCNAIR
astronaut

MALCOLM X
militant black leader

THURGOOD MARSHALL
Supreme Court justice

TONI MORRISON
author

ELIJAH MUHAMMAD
religious leader

EDDIE MURPHY
entertainer

JESSE OWENS
champion athlete

SATCHEL PAIGE
baseball great

CHARLIE PARKER
musician

GORDON PARKS
photographer

ROSA PARKS
civil rights leader

SIDNEY POITIER
actor

ADAM CLAYTON
POWELL, JR.
political leader

COLIN POWELL
military leader

LEONTYNE PRICE
opera singer

A. PHILIP RANDOLPH
labor leader

PAUL ROBESON
singer and actor

JACKIE ROBINSON
baseball great

DIANA ROSS
entertainer

BILL RUSSELL
basketball great

JOHN RUSSWURM
publisher

SOJOURNER TRUTH
antislavery activist

HARRIET TUBMAN
antislavery activist

NAT TURNER
slave revolt leader

DENMARK VESEY
slave revolt leader

ALICE WALKER
author

MADAM C. J. WALKER
entrepreneur

BOOKER T. WASHINGTON
educator and racial spokesman

IDA WELLS-BARNETT
civil rights leader

WALTER WHITE
civil rights leader

OPRAH WINFREY
entertainer

STEVIE WONDER
musician

RICHARD WRIGHT
author

ON
ACHIEVEMENT
❧

Coretta Scott King

BEFORE YOU BEGIN this book, I hope you will ask yourself what the word *excellence* means to you. I think that it's a question we should all ask, and keep asking as we grow older and change. Because the truest answer to it should never change. When you think of excellence, perhaps you think of success at work; or of becoming wealthy; or meeting the right person, getting married, and having a good family life.

Those important goals are worth striving for, but there is a better way to look at excellence. As Martin Luther King, Jr., said in one of his last sermons, "I want you to be first in love. I want you to be first in moral excellence. I want you to be first in generosity. If you want to be important, wonderful. If you want to be great, wonderful. But recognize that he who is greatest among you shall be your servant."

My husband, Martin Luther King, Jr., knew that the true meaning of achievement is service. When I met him, in 1952, he was already ordained as a Baptist preacher and was working toward a doctoral degree at Boston University. I was studying at the New England Conservatory and dreamed of accomplishments in music. We married a year later, and after I graduated the following year we moved to Montgomery, Alabama. We didn't know it then, but our notions of achievement were about to undergo a dramatic change.

You may have read or heard about what happened next. What began with the boycott of a local bus line grew into a national movement, and by the time he was assassinated in 1968 my husband had fashioned a black movement powerful enough to shatter forever the practice of racial segregation. What you may not have read about is where he got his method for resisting injustice without compromising his religious beliefs.

He adopted the strategy of nonviolence from a man of a different race, who lived in a different country, and even practiced a different religion. The man was Mahatma Gandhi, the great leader of India, who devoted his life to serving humanity in the spirit of love and nonviolence. It was in these principles that Martin discovered his method for social reform. More than anything else, those two principles were the key to his achievements.

This book is about black Americans who served society through the excellence of their achievements. It forms a part of the rich history of black men and women in America—a history of stunning accomplishments in every field of human endeavor, from literature and art to science, industry, education, diplomacy, athletics, jurisprudence, even polar exploration.

Not all of the people in this history had the same ideals, but I think you will find something that all of them had in common. Like Martin Luther King, Jr., they all decided to become "drum majors" and serve humanity. In that principle—whether it was expressed in books, inventions, or song—they found something outside themselves to use as a goal and a guide. Something that showed them a way to serve others, instead of only living for themselves.

Reading the stories of these courageous men and women not only helps us discover the principles that we will use to guide our own lives but also teaches us about our black heritage and about America itself. It is crucial for us to know the heroes and heroines of our history and to realize that the price we paid in our struggle for equality in America was dear. But we must also understand that we have gotten as far as we have partly because America's democratic system and ideals made it possible.

We are still struggling with racism and prejudice. But the great men and women in this series are a tribute to the spirit of our democratic ideals and the system in which they have flourished. And that makes their stories special and worth knowing.

1

A SUMMER DAY IN MAINE

❧

SUNDAY, JUNE 30, 1991, was a typically hot, humid summer day in Washington, D.C. But Judge Clarence Thomas of the U.S. Court of Appeals did not mind. He was content to be spending the afternoon working in his chambers. The night before, he and his wife, Virginia, had been celebrating—celebrating something that had not happened.

Anticipating the retirement of 83-year-old Supreme Court justice Thurgood Marshall, who was in poor health, representatives of President George Bush had indicated to Judge Thomas that he was being considered to take Marshall's place on the Court. But they cautioned him that if he was not nominated quickly when the time came, he would probably not be chosen at all. He had never been interviewed by the president about filling Marshall's seat.

At noon on Thursday, June 27, Marshall's letter of resignation had arrived at the White House. In addition to Thomas, other names immediately surfaced, including Judge Edith H. Jones, who had been seriously considered when another vacancy on the Court had occurred a year earlier. Thomas heard nothing that afternoon, nor the next day, nor the next.

As far as Thomas was concerned, no news was good news. At the age of 43, he had endured 11 years

A smiling Clarence Thomas meets reporters at the White House after being nominated for the post of associate justice of the Supreme Court in July 1991.

of public service that often reminded him of a firing range in which he was the principal target. Now, as a federal judge, he enjoyed lifetime tenure in an atmosphere of judicial peace and quiet, dealing with the kind of intellectual challenges he loved. Thomas had come farther than he ever dreamed possible, having grown up barefoot-poor in a marshy "colored town" called Pin Point, Georgia. He knew that without the stern discipline of his grandfather and the unyielding prodding of the Franciscan nuns who had taught him in the black parochial schools of Savannah, he might well have been one of the manacled prisoners he often saw from his office window.

A ringing telephone interrupted the Sunday silence of the office. One of Thomas's law clerks took the call, listened, and then handed the phone to Thomas. President Bush was on the line. He asked Thomas to get on a U.S. Air Force jet Monday morning and come to the Bushes' summer home at Kennebunkport, Maine.

When Thomas told his wife, Virginia, about the call, she shared his view that he was probably just being summoned to a courtesy interview, one of many the president would be conducting. But she also suggested that her husband prepare something to say to the media, just in case. "I am not going to be nominated," Thomas insisted.

But he sat at the kitchen table and jotted down some notes—just in case. Virginia Thomas said, "The only thing I'm going to tell you to put in it is—'Only in America.' "

Thomas arrived just before noon at the Bush home on Walker Point, a spit of land lapped on three sides by the Atlantic Ocean. The first person he met was First Lady Barbara Bush, who jarred his composure by blurting out, "Congratulations." Then she added, "Oops. I guess I let the cat out of the bag."

President Bush came to greet Thomas and led him through the kitchen, introducing him to staff members, then across a hallway into a combination bedroom–sitting room. After the two men were seated behind closed doors, Bush asked Thomas two questions.

"Will you and your family be able to make it through the confirmation process?" (All nominees for the Supreme Court must be approved by a majority of the U.S. Senate.)

"Yes, sir," Thomas said confidently. He had been before Senate committees for confirmation hearings four times in the previous nine years. Fifteen months earlier, he had endured a rough confrontation with the Judiciary Committee before his nomination to the Court of Appeals was confirmed. Thomas's well-known conservative views, while agreeable to the administration, had aroused strong opposition from liberal organizations and many members of Congress.

"Can you call them as you see them?" Bush asked.

"That's the way I've lived my life," Thomas said.

"Keep in mind," the president said, "you should not feel compelled to agree with me on anything. And any time you disagree with me, you won't ever hear me criticize you." Bush and Thomas did not discuss any controversial issues, such as abortion or the death penalty.

Bush ended the conversation by saying, "At two o'clock I will announce my intent to nominate you as an associate justice of the Supreme Court of the United States. Let's go have lunch."

"I about died," Thomas later told a friend. "It had gone from interviewing to being the nominee in about 20 minutes, and I am sitting there wondering, 'What happens next?' "

While a nervous Judge Thomas was lunching on crab salad with the president and his party on a porch overlooking the water, Thomas's mother, Leola Wil-

Leola Williams (right), Thomas's mother, in the midst of her duties as a nurse's aide at Candler Hospital in Savannah, Georgia. Upon learning that her son was about to undergo yet another difficult confirmation process for an important government post, Williams exclaimed, "Lord, not again."

liams, was grabbing a quick bite in the cafeteria at Candler Hospital in Savannah, Georgia, where she worked as a nurse's aide. Her shift was over, and as she passed the nursery on her way out, a coworker came out and said snidely, "Your son is not going to get the nomination. They've got two other people who will do just fine."

Leola turned to face the woman. "Lady, I care less. He's got a lifetime job and can take care of his family."

A friend patted Leola on the shoulder. "Let it roll off. She's jealous."

Leola hurried home; she had a second job taking care of a 105-year-old woman in the afternoons, and a third job working nights at a nursing home. When she got to her front door, the telephone was ringing. She opened the door, put down her purse, picked up the phone, and heard a friend's voice say, "Lee, you got your television on?"

"No. I just walked in the door."

"Well, turn it on. Your son is on it."

Leola turned on the set and saw her son Clarence standing behind President Bush on the lawn in Maine. She watched Clarence step toward the microphones and cameras, a crumpled piece of notepaper clutched tightly in his hand.

"As a child," he said, "I could not dare dream that I would ever see the Supreme Court, not to mention be nominated to it. In my view, only in America could this have been possible."

As he tried to thank his grandparents, his mother, and the nuns "who were so adamant that I grow up to make something of myself," he paused and gulped, as if he were trying to swallow a baseball. Reporters speculated that he was overwhelmed by the nomination itself. But they were wrong.

"It wasn't that," he said later. "It was this sudden rush of thoughts about my grandparents and neighbors and the nuns. This was an affirmation of all that they had taught me, and their belief that this was possible . . . you can do it. It did not have to be this high office. If I had become a schoolteacher, a priest, or just a good citizen with a coat-and-tie job, they would have been affirmed. But at the moment they saw me nominated to the Supreme Court of the United States, all that they had believed and all that they had accepted on faith was affirmed, and that's what I understood, and that's what that moment meant to me."

To Leola Williams, standing in the house where Clarence and his brother, Myers, had grown up, the moment meant something else. She raised her eyes toward heaven and called out, "Lord, not again. Do I have to go through this again with him?"

For the next 107 days, organizations and writers and commentators opposed to Thomas's nomination set out to dig up whatever they could find to use against him. Reporters by the hundreds retraced every step Thomas had ever taken on every path in his life, talking to everyone they could locate who had gone to school with him or worked with him or had even the slightest acquaintance with him. Computers retrieved thousands of pages of material recording everything that had ever been said, written, or thought by or about Clarence Thomas. Nothing was too trivial to be considered.

The process culminated in the most bitter, furious, and controversial confirmation hearing ever held by the Senate Judiciary Committee. When it was over, the Senate approved his appointment as the 106th associate justice of the Supreme Court by a vote of 52–48, the closest margin of approval in

Thomas is overcome with emotion as he and President George Bush announce his nomination to the Supreme Court. "As a child," he told the press, "I could not dare dream that I would ever see the Supreme Court, not to mention be nominated to it. . . . Only in America could this have been possible."

history. (Twenty-eight nominees had withdrawn or been rejected.)

At one point during the hearings, Thomas told the 14 senators on the committee facing him, "During the past 10 weeks, people have written and formed conclusions about me, and that has gotten to be a part of this process. I think they are free to do that. . . . But those conclusions that people formed about me were not the real Clarence Thomas." ⬤

2

PIN POINT

❧

A view of Savannah, Georgia, in the 19th century. When Clarence was six years old, he and his brother moved to Savannah to live with their mother, who had taken work cleaning houses. The family just scraped by on Leola's wages, sharing a single room in a run-down tenement.

I**T WAS A WARM**, pleasant evening in Pin Point, Georgia, on June 23, 1948. A light breeze carried the sweet smell of the nearby saltwater marsh into the little house where Leola Thomas stood in the light of a single bare overhead bulb, contentedly humming a hymn. She was expecting her second child soon, but her thoughts were on getting ready to attend a friend's wedding at the Sweet Fields of Eden Baptist Church just down the dirt road.

Suddenly she felt a sharp pain, followed quickly by another. She called to her aunt Annie Graham, whose house she shared with her husband and her daughter, Emma Mae. "Tell Uncle Charlie to go for the midwife," she said.

Uncle Charlie jumped in his truck and drove over to Sand Fly to get Lula Camp. Miss Lula delivered most of the babies born in the rural communities of Pin Point, Sand Fly, and White Bluff, which were located on the outskirts of Savannah. The midwife arrived, and at eight o'clock, she caught the emerging seven-pound infant in a pan made of folded newspaper. It was a difficult birth. "I always tease him, telling him his head was big," Leola said of the boy she named Clarence.

Clarence's father was M. C. Thomas, a farmer from Dublin, Georgia. Clarence scarcely got to know him. His parents divorced when Clarence was two, just before his little brother, Myers, was born. M. C. Thomas then moved to Philadelphia.

About 500 people lived in Pin Point, most in small wooden houses with no running water. Each family got water from a common pump in the yard. One outhouse served several families. Most of the houses were raised on red bricks or cinder blocks or—like Annie Graham's—slabs of wood cut from tree trunks. Aunt Annie's windows had no glass, just shutters. Inside, the uninsulated walls were covered with newspapers to keep out the wind. Clarence and Emma Mae often studied the advertisements and pictures of things they desired but did not have. The only books in the house were Sears and J. C. Penney catalogs—the wishing wells of the poor—and an old illustrated Bible. The children would lie on the wood floor for hours looking at the strange pictures in the Bible. One day as they were doing this, a little snake stuck its head up through a knothole in the floor and peeked around the room, scaring them half to death.

The yards of the houses were all neat and clean, bordered by white picket fences and filled with blossoms: hydrangeas, magnolias, azaleas, and big bunches of purple watermelon flowers. Tall pines and short palmettos competed for sunlight beneath a canopy of huge oaks and other trees, all of which were draped with the lacy gray Spanish moss that thrives in the South. Small vegetable gardens sprouted in the sandy soil.

Leola swept her yard with a broom made of the stiff grass that grew in the marshes. When Clarence was big enough, he raked the yard, often making an artistic pattern of lines in the dirt. He also helped his mother scrub the wooden floors with potash. Looking back 40 years later, he said, "I keep hearing this connection between disorder and poverty. We were poor but proud. You didn't see any disorder." His mother often reminded her children, "Just because you're poor, that doesn't mean you're nobody. You're always somebody."

The community's main employer, a crab- and oyster-packing plant named Varn & Son, stood beside Aunt Annie's house. On the dirt road in back of the house, a small cinder-block building served as a meeting hall for the Brotherhood of Friendship Society. Thurgood Marshall, in his days as a civil rights lawyer, once stopped to speak in the hall as he traveled through the South fighting segregation. A three-room schoolhouse sat opposite the Sweet Fields of Eden Church.

Most of the women of Pin Point worked at Varn & Son; others took the bus to Savannah, where they worked as maids, cooks, and cleaning women. Some men held jobs as day laborers or gardeners; others were watermen who raked oysters, fished, shrimped, and crabbed.

Leola Thomas was the fastest crab picker at Varn & Son, wielding a quick knife as she scooped out 50 to 75 pounds of meat from the shellfish that lay on the plant's long tables. "I could do 75 pounds if I sat there all day," she recalled with pride. "When I was pregnant with Clarence, I would go home and lie down for a while, then I'd go back and still beat them all."

The pickers earned five cents a pound. "We were going to strike for 10 cents, but when the man came in nobody said a word," Leola recalled. "They knew I was the one to shoot my mouth off, so they all looked at me and I spoke up and we got it. It's no wonder where Clarence got it from to speak his mind."

As they performed their monotonous, muscle-cramping chore hour after hour, the women often sang hymns. Outside, Clarence and his friends played; their shouts and laughter rang out against the sounds of "Father I Stretch My Hand to Thee," "The Help I Know," "Amazing Grace," and Leola's favorite, "Jesus Bears This Cross Alone."

Throughout his early childhood, Clarence never saw a store-bought toy. Running barefoot with his playmates, he caught minnows in the creeks and skipped shells across the water. When the tide was out, the fiddler crabs crawled into holes in the sand. The boys dug the crabs out with a stick; then they cut fishing poles from cane and used the little crabs as bait to catch sheepshead. They tied nets to catch shrimp (sometimes hauling in eels at the same time) and used the shrimp as bait for catfish.

If the children were lucky enough to find an abandoned tire, they climbed into it and gleefully rolled down the road. A discarded bicycle wheel provided hours of entertainment; they made it roll along by using a stick or a bent hanger, and when they tired of that, they took out the spokes and flung the wheel through the air with backspin, so that it landed in the dust and rolled back to them. They made trains from soda cans and fashioned skatemobiles from old skate wheels and stray pieces of wood. They manufactured baseballs by stuffing old stockings with the plentiful moss hanging from the trees. The girls made dolls out of broomgrass, putting Vaseline on the ends of the blades and curling it with a fork to form the doll's hair.

The children's favorite activity was shooting "pluffers." Every child had one. To make a pluffer, they would cut a 10-inch piece from the bamboo growing in the marshes and whittle a stick or a broom handle to a point so that it would fit inside the hollow center of the bamboo. The next step was to break off the neck of a bottle and place it over the end of the bamboo—this would cause a loud popping noise when the device was fired. For ammunition, the children picked green chinaberries from the trees. To fire the pluffer, a child would stuff two berries into the bamboo shaft and eject the first berry with a quick thrust of the stick. A good shot could travel up to 30 yards.

When he was not playing, Clarence earned a little money scrubbing crab barks, the back shells of the crabs, which were thrown into big tubs of water after the meat was cut out of them. He scrubbed the shells with a brush, rinsed them, and put them on a board to dry. The barks were then sold to restaurants to be used as serving dishes for deviled crab.

The children of Pin Point were raised on condensed milk, grits, butter, crabs, fish, and the greens and other vegetables grown in their gardens. Clarence was never ill; if he had been, there would have been no money for a doctor. His mother would have treated him with home remedies: fig leaves soaked in vinegar for a headache, sardine juice applied to swollen jaws for the mumps, and a dose of castor oil for a cold.

In addition to these remedies, there were superstitions that conveyed a moral code. As Leola recalled, "If you sassy an old person you'll have bad luck. . . . If you make a face at a pregnant woman, you are marking the baby, and it will turn out acting like the person who made the face." Later, she felt she had good reason to believe this last warning: "When I was pregnant with Clarence, my Daddy would make faces at me, and Clarence came out with a lot of Daddy's ways."

At Christmastime, the people of Pin Point decorated their houses with homemade paper bells and bright paper chains. Few had Christmas trees or presents. But they celebrated all the same; the children marched through the town beating on the bottoms of washtubs, scraping tin washboards with spoons, and pulling strings of empty cans through the dirt while whooping and hollering. This was the only time of year when the children got to taste the homemade scuppernong, peach, and pear wines enjoyed by the adults.

In Pin Point, everybody had a nickname. The nicknames, which might sound cruel or unflattering if used by an outsider, were really badges of acceptance and endearment. "Most blacks are given nicknames within their families when they are growing up," explained Doug Smith, a black writer. "It gives them something all their own to be proud of. It makes them special."

Leola had been dubbed Pigeon or Pidgie by her mother because her toes turned in when she walked.

A view of Savannah's West Broad Street during the 1950s. West Broad Street had once been a thriving black business district, but by the time of Clarence Thomas's childhood, most of the businesses had been taken over by whites.

Names such as Pig, Big Hawk, Big Brother, and Sister were engraved on tombstones in the Pin Point church cemetery. "I called Emma Mae Red because she was light-skinned," Leola said. "We called Clarence Boy and his brother, Myers, was Peanuts, although he weighed 13 pounds when he was born. Clarence's cousin Freddie Framble we called Nerves because his mother was always saying how her nerves were bothering her."

When Clarence was six, he put on shoes for the first time so that he could go to school. Wearing secondhand clothes collected by the church, he walked to the end of the lane and boarded the school bus. By this time, his mother had gone to live in Savannah, where she had found work as a cleaning woman. Aunt Annie Graham was caring for the three children. When Aunt Annie was at work and Emma Mae and Clarence were in school, little Myers was supposed to stay at his uncle's house next door. But he liked to wander. One morning, he went back into his own house. The big Jimbo wood-burning heater was red hot, and somehow a curtain caught on fire. Myers ran out just before the flames consumed the dry wood, the newspapers lining the walls, and everything else in the house.

Without a home in Pin Point, Leola brought her three children to Savannah. But Aunt Annie, who stayed behind with Uncle Charlie, cried over the loss of the only family she had ever had. So Leola sent Emma Mae back to Pin Point to live with Aunt Annie.

In Savannah, Leola earned $10 or $15 a week cleaning houses. On this salary, she could only afford one room in a tenement in a slum neighborhood near West Broadway, a black business street. She and the two boys had one bed, a bureau, a cheap love seat that Clarence slept on, and a kerosene stove that was usually cold. A lone window looked out on the busy street. Three other tenants lived in the building; they all used the same kitchen, which had an unreliable gas stove, no refrigerator, and worn linoleum covering a dirt floor. There was a filthy toilet in the backyard, but nobody used it. It had rusted out long before, and raw sewage leaked into the yard.

During the day, the boys ate cornflakes with watered-down condensed milk, along with the scraps of bread their mother brought home from her jobs. For the first time, Leola was on her own with children to look after. Without a telephone, there was no way she could supervise the boys while she worked. In the middle of the 1954–55 school year, just after the Supreme Court had ruled that segregated schools were unconstitutional, Leola enrolled Clarence in the afternoon session of the first grade at the all-black Florance Street School. But Clarence spent most of the time gazing out the classroom window, and after school he wandered the streets of Savannah.

Settled in 1733, Savannah is an old seaport on the Savannah River, 18 miles inland from the Atlantic Ocean. The first steamship to cross the Atlantic had left from Savannah in 1819. In the 1950s, the city's population was about 140,000. The main industry was the manufacture of paper for the brown bags used in supermarkets, and the acrid smell from the paper mills suffused the city.

Outside of the slum neighborhoods, Savannah's streets were lined with elegant old houses and massive oak trees. Peaceful shaded squares and small parks were everywhere. Downtown Savannah glittered with the lights of the new movie houses, and the department stores were filled with bright displays. But this was all part of the white world.

The Supreme Court's rulings against segregation had not disturbed the old ways. Even the tax records for blacks and whites were kept in separate books at the courthouse. Clarence dared not lift his head to

look at a white woman as he walked. Young black men had been lynched or sentenced to life in prison just for doing that. Blacks had to use separate water fountains and public rest rooms. Outside the black community, they could only get food only by going to the back door of a restaurant or to a window marked "Colored." If they tried something on in a white clothing or shoe store, they had to buy it even if it did not fit; white businessmen claimed they could not sell the item to a white person after a black had worn it. For this reason, Leola bought clothes two sizes too big for the boys and cut them down to be sure they would fit.

The Carnegie library on East Henry Street in Savannah. Because blacks were barred from the city's main library, young Clarence turned to the smaller Carnegie library to satisfy his love of reading.

Because of his skin color, Clarence could not enter the large public library, despite the enticing words that marched across the top of the building above the imposing white columns: "This Eternal Court Is Open to You with Its Society as Wide as the World."

Since the Civil War put an end to slavery, blacks had survived in Savannah. For a while, they had even prospered through self-reliance and solidarity. Before the Great Depression of the 1930s, there had been seven black-owned banks and many thriving businesses on East Broad and West Broad streets, the streets that bracketed most of the city. But by the 1950s, whites owned all the stores and businesses on those blocks, except for a few poolrooms and self-service laundries.

One day, Clarence came home from school with his head bloody. He told his mother that a group of boys had jumped on him and beat him up while a teacher stood by and did nothing. "I went to school and got all over that teacher," Leola recalled. "But he didn't know anything about it. They tried to find the boys who did it, but nobody had seen anything. Finally it came out that Clarence had been standing on a swing and swinging through the air when his feet slipped off. He held onto the chains but the swing flipped up and hit him in the head. He had made up that story because he did not like that school."

About that time, Leola remarried, and the family moved across town to a better house. The toilet was still outside, but at least it worked. Leola's new husband was willing to raise the boys, but Leola did not want any man outside her family to take care of them. So she asked her father, Myers Anderson, who lived a few blocks away, to take the boys to live with him. A hard-working, no-nonsense man, he said no.

"My mother had died when I was three," Leola recalled, "and Daddy had married a sweet angel of a woman named Christine, whom we all called Tina, or Teenie. She had never had any children, and she wanted Clarence and Myers so bad she told Daddy she would take the kids and if he didn't like it, he could move out."

So Clarence and Myers Thomas put everything they owned into two brown paper bags and reluc-tantly walked three blocks to their grandparents' home, a journey that had a more profound impact on their lives than anything else they ever did. •◊•

3

"OLD MAN CAN'T IS DEAD"

❦

Myers Anderson, Clarence's grandfather, was the most influential figure in his life. A man of deep pride and strong principles, Anderson imbued Clarence and his brother with an ethic of effort and achievement. "I was bequeathed a fortune in values and wise counsel," Clarence recalled.

MYERS ANDERSON WAS a tall, muscular man with large hands and a frown that would put the fear into a fussing child. The son of a jackleg (untrained) preacher whom he barely knew, Anderson had been raised by his mother, who died when he was nine years old. He then lived with his grandmother, who had been freed from slavery when she was a young girl. Myers was 12 when his grandmother died; he then went to live with an uncle who had about 20 children of his own.

Anderson left school after the third grade to work on the family farm and do "piecework" (working a plot of land for a white man). The most important lesson he learned came not from school but from what he saw of life: he learned that he would have to work hard to survive, without relying on the government or the white man for anything. That philosophy guided him in everything he did for the rest of his life.

As a young man, Anderson came to Savannah to work as a house mover for three dollars a week. Determined to make a life for himself independent of a white boss's whims, he bought an old truck from the man he worked for and went into business selling firewood. From that beginning, he expanded into hauling ice, kerosene, and coal. Later he bought a tanker truck to deliver heating oil and proudly had "Anderson Fuel Co." painted on the side of the truck. He worked seven days a week and never slept past dawn.

At one point, Anderson bought a machine to make cinder blocks, but the city would not give him a license to open a business. He sold the machine to a white man, who immediately went down to city hall and got the same license Anderson had been denied. But before he sold the machine, Anderson made enough cinder blocks to construct several houses, including the one he and Tina occupied when Clarence and Myers arrived in the summer of 1955.

When the two scared boys crossed the front porch and entered the house on East 32nd Street, their apprehension was overcome by wonder and awe. Tina and Daddy welcomed them into a comfortable living room that opened into a dining room. Beyond that they found their bedroom, which was equipped with twin beds and a desk. On the way, they passed a sparkling modern bathroom, the first they had ever seen. (Clarence and little Myers were so fascinated by the real indoor flush toilet, they would stand flushing it repeatedly, watching the swirling, gurgling water, until Daddy hollered at them to quit.) Off to the right was a spotless kitchen, big enough for a square table and four chairs. And best of all, they did not have to share the kitchen or bathroom with anybody else.

The boys soon learned that the comfort and luxury of their own room, indoor plumbing, and three good meals a day carried a price tag. "You're going to get up every morning early and work hard all day long," Daddy told them. "If you're not going to do that, you're going to leave."

Daddy did not want to hear them ever say they could not do something. Any problem could be solved with elbow grease. He also made it clear that he expected good manners and behavior in his house at all times. "He was not mean, he was fair," Clarence recalled. "He told you exactly what he was going to do and he did it. He always said, 'What's good for the gander is good for the goose,' and he treated me and my brother alike. There was no favoritism."

Daddy was as set in his ways as the sun. He expected a hot breakfast on the table every morning at 7:00, not 7:01; lunch at noon, not 12:05; supper at 5:00, not 5:15. If the boys slept past 7:00 on Saturday mornings, Daddy would yell to them through their window from the backyard, "Laziness is okay for the rich. Y'all think y'all are rich?"

Tina doted on the boys. Every day she had a hot breakfast waiting for them, while gospel music flowed from a little radio. She made their favorite foods— fried chicken, sweet potato pie, and greens. "If I was there at supper time," Leola Williams said, "I could sit in any chair but her boys' chairs. And I better not touch the pieces of chicken that were the boys' favorites."

Whenever the boys fought or got into mischief, Daddy would pull off his thick leather belt and dole out whippings. Tina intervened as often as she could. If Clarence and Myers acted up during the day, she would whip them lightly, then tell Daddy she had punished them severely. Sometimes she would call Leola to come and punish them. "When the boys saw me coming they'd run and hide under their beds," Leola said. "But Tina would tell me, 'No need to whip them. I already did it.' And Daddy would whisper to me, 'No, she didn't.' And of course she hadn't."

The house was situated in a quiet, safe neighborhood. Flowers and shrubbery bloomed in the well-kept yards. Every house was immaculate. On Saturday mornings, all the homeowners scrubbed their hardwood floors and porches and cut their grass. They all worked hard and scorned welfare. Once, a family on welfare moved onto the block. Their children ran wild, and rusting old cars and junk piled up in front of their house. The other residents looked down on the newcomers; being poor did not mean people had to abandon their standards or dignity. "Man ain't got no business on welfare as long as he can work," Daddy declared.

Discipline and caring permeated the neighborhood. Mr. Joe and Miss Bec lived behind the Andersons, Miss Maria next door, Miss Gladys next to her, then Mister "Hon' Chile," the Millers, and Miss Gertrude. They all looked out for each other's children and reported to Daddy or Tina if the boys got into mischief, such as the time they threw rocks through the glass roof of the florist's greenhouse across the street.

One day, Clarence and Myers crossed Henry Street, a busy thoroughfare, against the light. Miss Gertrude, whom Daddy described as "white-eyed" when she got too nosy, was sitting on a bus and saw the jaywalkers. She stuck her head out the window and cried, "I'm going to tell Tina." "We knew we were in trouble," Clarence recalled.

In Myers Anderson's view of life, God was central. Education, discipline, hard work, and knowing right from wrong held the highest priorities. Crime, welfare, alcohol, and laziness were the enemies. Daddy often reminded Clarence and Myers that his goal was to raise them so they could do for themselves, stand on their own two feet, and survive in spite of bigotry.

"My grandfather lived the Ten Commandments," Clarence later said. "And although everybody in that neighborhood had reason to be bitter, they were all devoutly religious. That's what gave them their grace and dignity. They would get upset about something they didn't think was fair, but they turned the other cheek and trusted in the Lord."

St. Benedict's School in Savannah, which Clarence Thomas began to attend in 1955, had been founded by Father Ignatius Lissner in 1907 with the specific aim of educating black youngsters and spreading the Catholic faith.

Although Clarence often thought his grandfather was too rigid and demanding and expected too much of him and Myers, he later realized, "I was bequeathed a fortune in values and wise counsel."

Daddy believed that education was the key to a better life. When he had moved to Savannah, he had gone to an integrated Catholic church, St. Benedict the Moor's, where he learned to read the Bible and follow the Mass in Latin. He then became a Catholic.

The diocese operated three elementary schools and a high school. St. Benedict's, a school for black boys, was run by white Franciscan nuns. Teaching in such a school could be hazardous for the nuns, because of the resentful whites who called them the "nigger sisters." One day, the Ku Klux Klan, a violent racist group, sent a hearse to the rectory next to the school as a warning to the nuns. When the sisters accompanied their students on the segregated public buses, they sat in the back with the boys, in the "colored" section.

In the fall of 1955, Daddy took Clarence to St. Benedict's and paid the $20 tuition for the year. He bought Clarence the ties, white shirts, and blue pants and sweaters that were the school uniform. "These are the rules," he told Clarence. "Your teachers are always right. Your grandmother's always right. If they beat you in school and you come home and complain about it, you'll get another one."

The Irish nuns in their brown habits maintained a discipline that inspired not only fear but respect. A stern scowl of disapproval could make a child cry. Anyone who misbehaved got whacked across the palm with a stick or ruler. At first, Clarence had a difficult time adjusting. Sister Mary Dolorosa, his second-grade teacher, gave him three D's, the only D's he ever got.

"It was a world of order," he said, "and that's exactly what we needed, because there was chaos all around us. Any punishment I got I deserved. We had large classes of 35 to 40 kids, but you could hear a pin drop in that school. They kept order; they could leave the room and there would still be order."

Despite the sisters' strictness, the boys saw a radiance in their faces that they knew was genuine. Sister Mary Virgilius Reidy, the principal, said, "They knew we wouldn't have been there if we didn't love the work and the children. We didn't believe the myths . . . that black children couldn't learn or didn't have the brains white children had."

Besides drilling the students in grammar, arithmetic, geography, and the other traditional subjects, the nuns imparted rules for success and imbued the children with large doses of confidence and self-esteem. "They made us believe that we were the equal of anybody," Clarence recalled, "and they gave us the same tests the white schools took. They refused to let us buy into the notion that we could never do well, despite all the stereotypes of inferiority around us. Today you have a different version of the same thing, that because of slavery or discrimination you can't do these things [if you're black]. Whether it's coming from a bigot who says blacks are unequal, or it's somebody who says, 'Oh, it's too bad blacks had all these things happen to them, so they can't do as well as whites,' the bottom line is exactly the same. But the nuns refused to let us believe that and give up."

Lester Johnson, a friend of Clarence's who attended St. Benedict's a few years later, remembered, "They were constantly telling us that we were very bright. Having someone white say that to us, when we were still using separate water fountains, was really something. We even tried to imitate their English, so there were a bunch of little black kids in Savannah running around speaking with Irish brogues."

On school days, Clarence put on his backpack and walked to the three-story, red-brick building—he missed only half a day in seven years. "The building was run down, the windows wouldn't close, and it was always cold inside," he later remembered. "But it was immaculate, inside and out. One crew of kids picked up the trash outside at lunch time, and another bunch picked up after school." Every morning the boys lined up around the flagpole on the small

Clarence (fourth from right) serves as an altar boy during Mass at St. Benedict's Catholic Church. Clarence valued the sometimes harsh discipline maintained by the priests and nuns because, he recalled, "It was a world of order, and that's exactly what we needed, because there was chaos all around us."

blacktop play area for the pledge of allegiance and the national anthem. Nothing that Clarence saw or heard was lost on him. Standing with a bunch of little black boys singing about "the land of the free," it struck him as odd that they were singing those words in a segregated world.

Thomas recalled that these solemn moments often gave way to comedy as the children slowly marched inside, two by two, beneath the ledges where the pigeons roosted. Whenever some unlucky student became a target for the birds, the other children laughed uproariously.

After school, Clarence learned to be an altar boy. By the time he was 13, he had earned the right to regularly serve at High Mass. Clarence also gained other highly prized honors, such as rolling up the flag when it was taken down and directing traffic as a patrol boy. But his mind was not always on school work or duties. He pulled as many tricks as he thought he could get away with. One day, he and two friends climbed one of the rusty iron fire escapes with a bag of sand. When one of the priests walked beneath them, they dumped the bag onto his head. None of the boys would say which one had done it, so they all stayed after school and cleaned the classrooms and the yard. When Daddy arrived at five o'clock, he sighed with exasperation, "You can lead a horse to water, but you can't make him drink."

Clarence and Myers got up to mischief at home, too. The railroad tracks crossed East 32nd Street near the Anderson house, and the freight trains slowed for the crossing. Clarence and Myers loved to run and catch hold of the train and climb into an open boxcar, then leap off before the train picked up speed again. One day the train accelerated too quickly and carried the boys far out of town before it slowed down enough for them to jump off. They had to walk all the way home. But this time they escaped punish-

ment; Daddy was laughing too hard at their story to reach for his belt.

After school, Clarence would race home and change his clothes so that he could do his chores around the house or help Daddy with the oil deliveries. Whenever he had any free time, he played sports, dreaming of becoming a professional basketball or football player. His biggest hero was Bob Hayes, the Olympic sprinter from Florida A & M. When Hayes was drafted as a receiver by the Dallas Cowboys, Clarence became a lifelong Cowboys fan. His basketball hero was the Boston Celtics star Bob Cousy. After reading that Cousy had practiced by

Bob Cousy of the Boston Celtics, shown dribbling past a defender in a 1957 contest, was one of Clarence's athletic heroes. Like many youngsters, Clarence often dreamed of becoming a professional basketball or football player.

shooting Ping-Pong balls into milk bottles, Clarence did the same thing. On the playground he practiced Cousy-style dribbling between his legs and behind his back until the other kids started calling him "Cous," a nickname that stuck through college.

Daddy and the boys watched all the sports they could find on the limited television schedules of the time. In the 1950s, the only baseball they saw was the Saturday afternoon "Game of the Week" and the World Series. They rooted for Willie Mays of the New York Giants and drank the chocolate drink he endorsed. In the fall, they picked up some Washington Redskins and Baltimore Colts games; their favorite players were Charlie Taylor and Johnny Unitas.

Daddy was a member of the National Association for the Advancement of Colored People (NAACP),

W. W. Law, Savannah's most prominent civil rights leader, believed that education was the key to bettering the lot of black people in the South. For this reason, Law and other adults repeatedly urged Clarence to work hard at school and improve his grades.

the nation's leading civil rights organization. Sometimes he took Clarence to the NAACP meetings on Sunday afternoons and proudly read off Clarence's report card grades. The local NAACP leader, W. W. Law, would praise Clarence for doing well in school, at the same time exhorting him to do even better. The black adults Clarence came into contact with impressed on him that nothing was more important than education if he hoped to lead a better life than they had. He never received a nickel or a dime reward for doing something without being admonished to "get your education." "Once you get something up here," people would say, pointing to his head, "no one can take it away from you."

Clarence was seven when he and Myers celebrated their first Christmas at Daddy's house. When they woke up on Christmas morning, they found a set of electric trains, their first real present. The next year, Clarence received his first bicycle, a bright red Western Flyer with a fender that flared out. The boys were also given skates and cap guns and enjoyed all these new wonders of life.

Clarence developed his lifelong love of books when he discovered the small Carnegie library for blacks a few blocks from home on East Henry Street. (Beginning in the 1880s, the wealthy industrialist Andrew Carnegie financed the building of nearly 1,700 libraries throughout the United States.) Although he could not take out books from the main library, he took to heart the motto displayed above its doors: "Oh Make Books Thy Comrades." The first time Clarence entered the children's section in the basement of the little red-brick building, the sight of a room filled with books fascinated him. He wanted to read everything he saw. He began by devouring every Dr. Seuss book he could get. Soon he turned to sports fiction, such as *Crazy Legs McBain*. He then discovered comic books at Mr. Lee's store on East

Broad Street. Despite his grandfather's disapproval, he bought "Two-Gun Kid," "Rawhide," and "Kid Cole," read them avidly, and eagerly awaited the next issues. He also read sports magazines, especially enjoying the stories about Bob Hayes.

"Nobody I knew, nobody in my neighborhood read," Clarence recalled. "I just started reading because I read about things I liked." When he reached the fourth grade, he was allowed to use the adult section of the library. There he became hooked on C. S. Forester's novels about the adventures of Captain Horatio Hornblower. "I didn't like the water myself," he confessed, "but reading about how they handled the ships during storms, and all their adventures out on the ocean, it was like you got on this magic carpet and zoomed off to another world. It took me out of that segregated library in the segregated South. You could go any place, do anything, dream and imagine." If Clarence wanted a particular book, the Carnegie librarians would send for it from the main library. He became their best customer, and he never forgot their kindness and encouragement. Whenever he became upset about something or grew resentful of his grandfather's relentless demands, he headed for the library: "It was quiet there, and I would just sit there and flip through an old encyclopedia or look at the pictures in magazines and think: one day I'm going to be able to read all these magazines and big books."

When the library closed at nine o'clock, he went home with a book in his hands. Until he went away to school, he did his homework at the kitchen table or at the desk in his room, often listening to the Supremes, the Temptations, and Martha and the Vandellas on radio station WSOK.

When Clarence was nine years old, he saw his father again briefly, in the projects where his mother lived. But there was no bond between them, and

M. C. Thomas remained a stranger to his son until many years later, when Clarence was a man. At that point, Clarence and M. C. began to spend more time together, and Clarence never bore any animosity toward his father because of his absence in the past.

During this time, Clarence had his first look at the world beyond Pin Point and Savannah. Daddy took him in the car on a trip north to Philadelphia, where they visited Daddy's sister. Then they went to New York City to visit Tina's sister. Clarence learned to play stickball in the city streets, and he saw electric-powered buses for the first time.

Back home, he also learned more about hard work. One day during the Christmas holiday in 1957, the whole family piled into Daddy's car and rode 29

A farmer cultivates young cotton plants in the rural South. Clarence and his brother, Myers, spent many summers helping out on the Anderson family farm; Clarence especially liked to ride the tractor because the quiet and solitude of the fields gave him time to think.

miles to the Anderson family farm in Liberty County. Working on weekends and holidays, Daddy and the boys, aided by some bricklayers, built a cinder-block house in five months. Then they cleared the land to plant corn, watermelons, collards, rice, and beans. From then on, the boys spent every summer on the farm, where it was cooler than in the city.

Clarence later said of his days on the farm, "I have never worked so hard for so little in all my life." But if the boys complained, Daddy reminded them, "You can't reap what you don't sow."

On the farm, the boys helped build garages and barns, and they strung a wire fence around the 72 acres. They picked beans until their backs ached, picked corn in the August heat, cleared trees and underbrush, and cut sugarcane until their hands were a mass of blisters. When Daddy plowed the fields with a horse or a mule, Clarence and Myers trudged along behind him. They took care of the chickens, pigs, and cows. They worked from sunup to sundown, resting only when Daddy took a nap after lunch. The boys took advantage of the break to throw rocks at cousin Jack Fuller's horse, Lizzie, and to look for alligators in the ditches. If nothing else, the hard life of a farmer taught Clarence "to value education." He was saved from boredom by the Carnegie librarian from Savannah, Mrs. Cameron, who came to the local church every Sunday with an armful of books and took back those he had read during the week.

When Clarence was 13, Daddy bought an old Ford tractor and turned the plowing over to the boys. They also used the machine to haul logs and rake hay. Riding alone on the tractor during the monotonous circuit of the fields gave Clarence time to reflect. "Usually I would think about a world that was unlike the one we were supposed to live in," he said in a 1986 speech. "I would wonder about the tremendous contradictions and discrepancies between the way we live and the way our Constitution and Bill of Rights read. . . . I wondered why the church and schools were segregated. Weren't we all equal in the eyes of God?"

When Clarence experienced racial prejudice first-hand, it blistered his soul the way cutting cane rubbed his hands raw. One day at the farm, a big car approached along the dirt road, sending up a huge cloud of dust. Clarence and Myers ran to the road as Daddy came out of the field to see who was coming. When the car stopped, a white woman leaned out the window and addressed Daddy as "Boy."

"You could see him seethe," Clarence recalled. "He looked around and saw his little kids there. People say, 'What kind of manhood does it take to yell back and get mad?' But what must it have taken for him not only to take the insult, but the stares from his kids seeing him being called a boy."

The family had to endure many other slights. One day, they were driving to the farm when Daddy noticed that the gas gauge was close to reading empty. He pulled into a service station, but before he filled up he asked the owner, a white man, if Tina could use the rest room. "We have no colored rest room," the man said, refusing to let Tina use the one for whites. The only alternative was to go around back of the building. Daddy angrily told the man he could keep his gasoline. He drove on and luckily found a station with rest rooms for blacks before the car ran out of gas.

Daddy refused to let discrimination or humiliation destroy his dignity. Determined to lead a decent life despite the abuse and indignities inflicted on black people, he remained a fair-minded, generous man. He gave away produce from the farm and bought groceries for people who had no money. He sometimes delivered heating oil to St. Benedict's without asking for payment. He and Tina believed that their examples would instill in Clarence and Myers a determination to work hard, to be good citizens, and to be fair.

In an article on Thomas, Jack E. White, the first black senior editor at *Time* magazine, reminisced about growing up with a similar grandfather: "You don't have to delve into the history of any successful black American to find someone like . . . Myers Anderson . . . who taught that hard work and self-reliance could overcome any obstacle discrimination might put in his way—if he was willing to pay the price." Clarence often felt that his grandparents' expectations were too high, but when he heard a preacher say they were "money poor but value rich," he could only respond, "Amen."

When 10-year-old Clarence reached the fifth grade, he felt very grown up; the fifth-grade classroom was upstairs at St. Benedict's. Each year he loved and

Clarence (second row, second from left) poses with schoolmates at St. Benedict's during a school ceremony. Throughout Clarence's school years, his dedicated teachers pushed him to realize his potential.

appreciated his teachers more. His favorite was Sister Mary Virgilius Reidy, the principal, who also taught sixth grade. She pushed him harder than he had ever been pushed. "She made it clear that I had more talent than I displayed," he said, "and she would accept no excuses." "Clarence was a B-plus student," Sister Mary recalled. "He was bright, ordinary, mischievous, not a genius, but hardworking and always polite."

Clarence had two cousins who were students at Savannah State College. Sometimes he would strain to imagine what the incredible world of college was like, a world that seemed so far away and nearly unattainable to a youngster still in elementary school. He envied the older students he saw waiting for the bus with their heavy burden of books, and he aspired to nothing more glorious than to be one of them.

Together, the nuns of St. Benedict's and the local librarians kept the flames of learning and ambition burning bright in Clarence Thomas. They overcame the negative feelings that washed over him whenever he mouthed the words "the land of the free," even as he knew he could not go to a James Bond movie because it was showing at a whites-only theater.

Every time doubts crept into his mind, the words of Myers Anderson shooed them away: "Old man can't is dead. I helped bury him." •◐•

4

"INTEGRATION SHOCK"

❦

T HE 5-FOOT-2-INCH, 98-pound Clarence Thomas entered all-black St. Pius X High School for the ninth grade in September 1962. The nuns' demanding standards continued: pulled ears, tugs on the shoulders, rulers whacked across palms, and the stern reprimand, "Don't you dare look at me in that tone of voice."

The students rebelled in subtle ways. Girls' dresses, for example, which had to end two inches below the knees in school, mysteriously rose to three inches above the knees after school.

At home, Clarence became a know-it-all. Feeling his oats or, as Tina called it, "smelling his musk," he sneered at the idea of uneducated people like his grandparents presuming to tell him anything. In school, however, he showed a sudden lack of effort that perturbed the sisters. The nuns, who cared about their students as if each one was the only child in their charge, stubbornly refused to let him give up on himself.

Meanwhile, Clarence was fielding prejudice from all sides. While whites considered him invisible unless he tried to enter their world, blacks created a cruel caste system of their own, based ironically on the same immutable fact of skin color. Other black

Thomas poses with fellow graduates of St. John's Seminary. As the only black student in an all-white school, Thomas worked extra hard to prove that he was intellectually equal to his classmates.

youngsters taunted him because he was darker than most and had short, fuzzy hair—"nigger naps," they called it. "ABC" was another frequent nickname, meaning "America's Blackest Child."

Clarence's dilemma was far from unique. Brenda Tapia, who enrolled in Washington's Howard University, a predominantly black school, to escape the white racism of the South, had a similar experience. "I was the wrong shade of black," she said. "At Howard if you were not light, bright, pretty near white and sitting on your hair, you were likely to experience a lot of prejudice [from other blacks]. . . . I got in a thing about hating black people, and that is a pretty difficult place to be. When you hate white people and you hate black people you get kind of lonely."

But the double-barreled derision did not create hatred in Clarence. Instead, it reinforced his focus on his own inner resources and integrity. When he completed the 10th grade, the snide comments written by other students in his yearbook brought him to a resolution. As he later recalled, he decided "then and there at the ripe old age of 16 that it was better to be respected than liked. Popularity is unpredictable and vacillating. Respect is constant."

He had read a Robert Frost poem, "The Road Not Taken," and it became a signpost for the rest of his life. Frost's poem ends: "I shall be telling this with a sigh / Somewhere ages and ages hence: / Two roads diverged in a wood, and I— / I took the one less traveled by, / And that has made all the difference."

During the early 1960s, the civil rights movement was sweeping segregation from southern life. The black citizens of Savannah, led by W. W. Law and Hosea Williams, united in a 16-month boycott of white businesses. They staged sit-ins and voter registration drives. In many southern cities, these efforts were met with violence. But Savannah city officials sought to avoid the turmoil that was tearing apart so much of the South. One hundred years earlier, during the Civil War, their ancestors had negotiated with General William Tecumseh Sherman to spare the city from being destroyed by the Union army on its march through Georgia. In the same spirit, white leaders met with Savannah's blacks in the summer of 1963 and peacefully agreed to desegregate public places such as theaters, restaurants, hotels, and rest rooms. The schools, however, remained as they were. (Unfortunately, many black-owned stores and restaurants were casualties of integration—now that black customers were welcome in the white establishments downtown, the black businesses lost their essential role in the community, and many were forced to close.)

Myers Anderson, a registered Democrat, had worked for civil rights as an active member of the NAACP. In his practical, hardheaded way, he under-

Civil rights leader Hosea Williams (center) led the fight for equality in Savannah during the early 1960s. Responding to black protests, the city leaders agreed to desegregate all public facilities, except schools.

stood that there would always be garden-variety racism and slights. But he did not believe that this should determine or define a black man's life. He and Tina had risen above injustice, and he believed that Clarence and Myers held the power in their own hands to educate themselves and work for a better life than his own generation had known.

The struggles, determination, and courage of the Myers Andersons of the nation led to the passage of the Civil Rights Act of 1964, which banned discrimination in public places throughout the nation, and to the passage of the Voting Rights Act in 1965. The civil rights activists thus accomplished much of what they had set out to do, creating unprecedented opportunities for their children and grandchildren. The color of their skin no longer had to limit their aspirations. The next step was to see that those opportunities were not wasted by inadequate preparation.

In 1959, the Catholic diocese had opened St. John Vianney Minor Seminary, a boarding school for boys about 10 miles outside Savannah on the Isle of Hope. The school consisted of a few plain yellow one-story cinder-block buildings containing classrooms, dorms, and a dining room. There was no indoor gym, just a blacktop basketball court and a sandy field for touch football and softball games. Pine trees lined one side of the playing field; giant oaks marched along the others. A tan wooden church rested on cinder blocks a few hundred yards beyond the field. The church had a stumpy steeple and plain windows; its only impressive feature was the oaks towering over it.

One Sunday night in September 1964, Myers Anderson took Clarence to the Isle of Hope, where he joined 27 other sophomores. Though he had already completed two years of high school, Clarence was thinking of becoming a priest and he had not yet taken the Latin courses he would need to get into a major seminary. Thus, he had to repeat the 10th grade. "Repeating the 10th grade was the best thing for me," he recalled. "It gave me a year to be older than my classmates, and to repeat some subjects like geometry."

Clarence later said that when he entered the dormitory building and was shown to his room, "I about died." He saw 14 narrow beds alternating with 14 small bureaus, some lined up along the walls and others filling the middle of the room, a jolting change from the comfortable privacy of the room he had shared with his brother. He also discovered that there was only one other black student in the school. (That student did not return the following year.)

Daddy had warned Clarence, "They're going to be watching you because you're black. You go there

Thomas compares notes with a fellow student at St. John's. One of the best students at the junior seminary, Thomas consistently earned A's and B's in all his courses.

and do us proud." Integration provided opportunities, but it also carried with it vulnerability to being hurt and rejected by the white world that Clarence was being thrust into for the first time. Most white youths had grown up among adults who espoused the idea that blacks were inferior to whites. Most of the boys bore no malice and did not think of themselves as prejudiced. To them, white superiority was just a fact of life.

On the whole, Clarence had no problem fitting in with the boys at St. John's. He got along fine with virtually everyone. As is true of any group, there were a few who made occasional biting remarks. The deepest hurt Clarence experienced came from something that was *not* said. One night, in the darkened dorm room, one boy yelled out, "Smile, Clarence, so we can see you." The crude remark itself did not bother Clarence—he had heard worse, from blacks and whites alike. What hurt him was that nobody else told the taunter to shut up. None of Clarence's friends stood up for him. Like all youngsters, he had been told the old adage "Sticks and stones may break my bones, but names will never hurt me." Now he realized that silence could be painful too.

The effects of leaving a nurturing black environment and being suddenly immersed in an indifferent white world were later labeled "integration shock." As part of that first wave of young blacks sent out to integrate America, Clarence found that it could be lonely in the vanguard. He was not totally accepted by whites, and he was no longer "in" with blacks. His black friends in town teased him about going to the white school, "St. John's the Cemetery." On the other side, a white student wrote in his sophomore yearbook, "Keep on trying, Clarence. Someday you'll be as good as us." Clarence thought, Well, we'll see. "It offended me," he later said, "but it told me that I had to keep running to catch up."

Thomas takes a healthy cut during an intramural baseball game at St. John's. In addition to his fine academic performance, Thomas excelled at baseball, football, basketball, and track.

At St. John's, the boys had Thursday afternoons off. Clarence would go home, but he spent the time studying. When the others went into Savannah during their leisure time, he stayed at school and hit the books. After lights out, he sneaked into the bathroom to read or pulled the blanket over his head and read with a flashlight. In addition to textbooks, he read 50 pages a night of Margaret Mitchell's saga of the Old South, *Gone with the Wind*.

Sister Mary Carmine, a teacher at St. Pius X High School, taught Clarence's chemistry class at St. John's. She brought him an old typewriter from Pius, and Clarence practiced an hour a day until he became a speedy typist. Under the continual prodding of his teachers, he did well in his studies, earning A's and B's. In the school's yearbook, *The Grail*, his academic work was recognized with the comment, "Blew that test, only a 98."

Clarence was the best athlete at St. John's. The school newspaper, the *Pioneer*, described him as

As coeditor of the Pioneer, his high school newspaper, Thomas spoke out against all forms of intolerance. "I think races would fare better if extremists would crawl back into their holes," he wrote in one of his editorials.

"faster than a speedy spitball . . . more powerful than home brew." Playing quarterback, Clarence led his eight-man football team, the Cowboys, to the school championship. The *Pioneer* praised his "superb throwing and elusive footwork." Clarence's receiver, Bennie Swiderek, caught 14 touchdown passes that fall.

Clarence was also the captain and leading scorer of the school basketball team, nicknamed the Lllamas. (Clarence's classmate Steve Seyfried chose the name because, he said, "a 3-L llama is a big fire"). In the annual school Olympics, Clarence won the baseball-, softball-, and football-throwing competitions—his distance in the softball event was 273.6 feet. He also won the standing and running broad jumps, leaping 17 feet, 7 inches in the latter.

Clarence also appeared in the school's production of *Mr. Roberts*, speaking two lines in the role of a shore-patrol officer. The next year, he worked on the sets for a production of *The King and I*, for which Tina helped sew the costumes.

One year, Clarence was coeditor of the *Pioneer*. The spirit of independence—in thought and action—so deeply instilled in him by his grandfather came through in a column he wrote when he was 18. Reflecting on the violence and hatred that gripped the country following the passage of the Civil Rights Act of 1964, he wondered why blacks and whites seemed unable to live in harmony, and offered a solution that presaged his thoughts of 25 years later:

I think races would fare better if extremists would crawl back into their holes, and let the people, whom this will really affect, do just a little thinking for themselves, rather than follow the Judas goats of society into the slaughter pens of destruction. True, the intellectuals must start the ball rolling, but ignorance in the intelligentsia is not unheard of. . . . It's about time for the average American to rise from his easy chair and do what he really and truly believes God demands of him—time to peel off the veil of hate and contempt, and don the cloak of love (black for white and white for black).

At times Clarence felt discouraged about race relations, certain that no matter how many legal barriers fell, no matter how much he excelled in the classroom or on the playing field, there was nothing a black man could do to be accepted by whites. Integration was supposed to emphasize people's commonality of purpose and potential, downplaying their differences. But it did not seem to be working that way, not as long as a classmate could write to him, "Clarence, you did very well in spite of being black."

Only his grandfather's example and the nuns' steely determination prevented Clarence from sinking into a quagmire of self-doubt. At a reunion 20 years later, Clarence saluted the sisters who had taught him: "There was no way I could have survived if it had not been for the nuns . . . who made me pray when I didn't want to and didn't know why I should—who made me work when I saw no reason to—who made me believe in the equality of races when our country paid lip service to equality and our church tolerated inequality—who made me accept responsibility for my own acts when I looked for excuses. . . . Without our nuns, I would not have made it to square one."

After graduating from high school in 1967, Clarence worked with a white schoolmate, John Scherer, as a counselor at a summer camp on the school grounds. Every morning after Mass, the campers gathered around the flagpole for the pledge of allegiance. Clarence and John stood together, and following the words "with liberty and justice for all," they added softly, "sometimes." "It was our way of acknowledging that the ideal was not the reality for many people," Scherer recalled.

The flagrant prejudice that had been displayed by some of his classmates at St. John's perplexed

Mourners surround the coffin of the Reverend Martin Luther King, Jr., in Atlanta in April 1968. Comments about the assassination made by Thomas's seminary classmates were a major factor in his decision to leave the seminary.

Clarence. He wondered how they could call themselves Christians while holding such attitudes toward other people. Despite these misgivings, he intended to become a priest.

In the fall of 1967, Clarence entered Immaculate Conception Seminary in northwestern Missouri. One of a handful of black students in his class, he had no problem settling in, never standing out as the best or the worst in the classroom. He refused to wear the face of the victim of injustice, smothering whites with feelings of guilt. In general, he got along fine, although there were occasional racial slurs. "I was determined not to see every slight or criticism as discrimination or bigotry," he later said. "Once you get into the habit of doing that, you disempower yourself; your attitude becomes: No matter what I do, discrimination will prevent me from doing well. I knew bigotry, but I refused to attribute everything to that."

In keeping with Myers Anderson's lessons of self-reliance, Clarence believed that he would succeed or fail by his own efforts. But he became further disenchanted with a Catholicism that tolerated open expressions of prejudice. Back in Savannah during Christmas vacation, he told his parish priest that he did not think the seminary was right for him. He expressed his concern that the church was not moving ahead to combat discrimination. He discussed his doubts with Tina but returned to Immaculate Conception determined to give it his best shot.

The last straw came on April 4, 1968, the day the Reverend Martin Luther King, Jr., was shot by an assassin. When the news was announced, Clarence recalled, "I was following this white seminarian up a flight of stairs, and I overheard him say, 'That's good. I hope the SOB dies.' I knew I couldn't stay in this so-called Christian environment any longer."

Myers Anderson was upset when Clarence declared that he was leaving the seminary. He had taken pride in the prospect of having a priest in the family. Moreover, he was displeased that Clarence was not going to finish something he had started. "I had given my word," Clarence later said, "but after major soul-searching, I regretfully concluded it was the right decision for me."

Clarence was tired of the hassles and degradation that came with being one of the few blacks in an all-white school. While working that summer at the Union Camp bag factory in Savannah, he considered enrolling at Savannah State, the small black college his cousins had attended. But Sister Mary Carmine had other ideas. ❦

5

THE MAKING OF AN INDIVIDUAL

🙚🙠

A view of the library at the College of the Holy Cross in Worcester, Massachusetts. When Thomas began his studies at Holy Cross in 1968, he was one of only six black students in the freshman class.

THE TENACIOUS SISTER Mary Carmine was not about to abandon the cause of Clarence Thomas, whom she believed capable of more than he envisioned for himself. She wanted to see him go to the College of the Holy Cross, a Jesuit school in Worcester, Massachusetts. Throughout the summer of 1964, she urged Thomas to send for the application forms, but he was not interested. He applied to the University of Missouri and was accepted.

Undaunted, Sister Mary Carmine wrote to one of her former students, Bob DeShay, who was at Holy Cross, and asked him to send the forms to Thomas. Then she kept after Thomas until he reluctantly filled them out. He was accepted; he still did not want to go to a "white" school—there would be only six blacks in his class—but he was no match for the iron will of the determined Franciscan sister. So, in September, he boarded a train headed north, carrying $100 stashed in his shoes, a box of Tina's fried chicken, and a head filled with doubts and uncertainties.

The handsome, white-trimmed red-brick buildings of the Holy Cross campus sat high on a hill overlooking Worcester, a declining factory town. Thomas felt as if he had been transported to another world. "It had to be hard coming up as a black from the South and into the northeastern community with a heavy population from Boston," reflected the Reverend John E. Brooks, vice-president of the school. "But he didn't let it throw him at all."

Although Thomas was surprised by the frequency of racial slurs he heard in the North, he had no problems personally. "Nobody ever did anything to me. I got along just fine." One incident that did throw him occurred when he bought a Sunday *New York Times* from a vendor; when he complained that the comics section was missing, the vendor informed him that the *Times* never printed any comics.

Thomas quickly realized that the school's efforts to attract black students had put a mark on him as surely as if a *T* for "tokenism" had been branded on his forehead. To many whites, he and the 24 other blacks at Holy Cross were there not because they deserved to be but just because they were black. Indeed, in some cases it was true. Thomas witnessed the high dropout rate of blacks who were not up to the academic challenge. Some gave in to the self-doubt and anxiety that integration had thrust upon them: they displayed an aversion to learning, cut classes, and made little effort. It was their way of shrinking from the challenge for fear that trying and failing would just confirm their own uncertainties and the widely held belief in their inferiority.

Their spirits broken, the dropouts complained that the school had crushed them. Thomas's firsthand observations led to his later firm and fiercely criticized opposition to affirmative action programs, which gave blacks preferential treatment regardless of their qualifications. "I watched the operation of such . . . policies when I was in college," he later told the *New York Times*, "and I watched the destruction of many kids as a result. It was wrong for those kids, and it was wrong to give that kind of false hope."

The dismay and defeatism around him were infectious. The steady drone of complaints—"They won't let us do this . . . you can't do that"—began to suffocate him. "Why make the effort?" some said. "They're all against us." But the competing voice of Myers Anderson would not be hushed: "You can't do better than I did without education. . . . Once you have it up here [in your head] they can't take it away from you." "Somehow," Thomas reflected, "[the older generation] knew intuitively that it was better to be educated without knowing where it would lead than to be uneducated." Making the effort meant occasional failures, but that risk could not be allowed to deter him from trying.

By nature a very quiet student in the classroom, Thomas sat in the back and rarely asked a question. Although he wanted to be judged by his work and not for doing well "for a black man," his silence in class derived from a different problem. "One reason for my being inconspicuous was that I had difficulty speaking proper English," he later said. "I would think about the right way to phrase a question while I was trying to say it, and trip over myself. Some people thought I had a stuttering problem. So I remained quiet."

Aware of his deficiency, he majored in English; he knew that speaking correctly and being able to express himself clearly and effectively would be essential to success in whatever he did. He studied long and hard, remembering what Martin Luther King, Jr., had once told a group of students: "When you are behind in a footrace, the only way to get ahead is to run faster than the man in front of you. So when your white roommate says he's tired and goes to sleep, you stay up and burn the midnight oil."

While some black students complained because they could not afford to travel during spring breaks as the whites did, Thomas saw it as an opportunity

Malcolm X, photographed during a 1963 rally in Harlem, exerted a powerful influence on Thomas's thinking during his college years.

to do the catching up that King had described. But he was not a total grind. He played some intramural football and basketball and ran sprints on the track team. Off campus, he worked at a free breakfast program for black youths. He also worked in the dining hall to earn some much-needed spending money. In the dorms, he enjoyed the all-night rap sessions, often taking an unpopular view just for the mental exercise. He studied Malcolm X, Booker T. Washington, and the Black Panthers, taking something from each of these diverse sources to develop his own philosophy.

During the late 1960s, college students were increasingly protesting against the Vietnam War and U.S. investments in South Africa. Thomas was not in the forefront of the protests. He wore the combat boots and army fatigues that were the trademark of campus radicals, but that was more to get through the snow and ice of the northern winters than to make a statement of any kind. Nevertheless, he would not let an injustice pass when it hurt his friends.

In December 1969, a group of Holy Cross students demonstrated against the school's investments in South Africa, then ruled by a minority white government that brutally oppressed the nation's nonwhite population. The few blacks who took part in the protest were more readily identifiable than the whites and bore the brunt of the suspensions handed out by the school. This was one of the difficulties of being in a predominantly white environment.

"Nothing had happened to me personally," Thomas recalled, "but my friends were being treated unfairly. So I stood up for them, and we all started to walk off the campus." But while he was walking out, he envisioned himself packing his trunk and showing up at his grandfather's front door unexpectedly in the middle of his junior year. "I asked myself: I have a straight A average; why am I walking out? And how do I explain what I am doing to my grandfather, to whom education means everything, if I am suspended from school, too? I was very happy when Father Brooks helped to resolve the problem and allowed us all to return."

The slogans of "black power" were also heard throughout the land at that time, as groups such as the Black Panthers urged blacks to reject the American political system and create a revolution. But the pursuit of power as an end in itself held no allure for Thomas. He reasoned that defining himself by skin color was exactly what white people had been doing to blacks for centuries; why should he now do the same thing to himself?

At the time, Afro hairstyles were the vogue. Thomas let his hair grow out for a while, then had it trimmed. "You aren't truly black if you don't wear an

Afro," he was told, but he dismissed the remark. "I certainly didn't define myself through my barber," he observed.

Above all, Thomas strove to be true to his own beliefs and resisted being submerged into a collective black voice. Black power advocates aimed at enfranchising him because he was black, but Thomas wanted to be judged for his own qualities. He wove into his cloak of identity what Shelby Steele wrote of Martin Luther King, Jr., in *The Content of Our Character*: "King understood that racial power subverts moral power, and he pushed the principles of fairness and equality rather than black power because he believed those principles would bring blacks their

Demonstrators protesting U.S. military action in Vietnam confront military police in Washington, D.C., in 1967. Although Thomas was surrounded by radical ferment during his college years, he always counseled moderation.

most complete liberation. . . . What made King the most powerful and extraordinary black leader of this century was not his race but his morality."

Thomas also agreed with Ralph Ellison, who wrote in his award-winning novel *Invisible Man*, "Our task is that of making ourselves individuals. The conscience of a race is the gift of its individuals."

Thomas felt that black power advocates, assuming the role of victims, were looking for an easy way to feel morally superior to whites. He was repelled by their slogan "Black Is Beautiful" (as long as one was not *too* black), their claim that blackness is virtue and whiteness is evil, and their overall self-righteousness. His beliefs caused some critics to later accuse him of running away from his black identity. But when black political causes clashed with the ideals he had been taught by his grandfather, he distanced himself from those causes and remained loyal to the principles of Myers Anderson.

Unlike most other black students at Holy Cross Thomas did not feel the need to stand apart from the rest of the campus. But he did help them start the Black Students Union, serving as its first treasurer and later losing a close election for president. He was neither a firebrand leader nor a blind follower, but an independent thinker and a voice of moderation.

Thomas demonstrated these qualities in the spring of 1969, when the black students decided they wanted their own separate section in the dormitory. Thomas preferred to be part of the whole academic community. He had many white friends. Since his arrival at Holy Cross, he had not allowed anger and hostility to dominate his relations with white students, and he did not intend to start now. "If one is at Holy Cross," he said, "he should profit from the experience by learning to associate with and understand the white majority."

At the time, Thomas's roommate was John Siraco, a white biology major who went on to medical school. Siraco and Thomas treated each other as equals and learned from each other. Their warm and valued relationship was one reason Thomas opposed self-segregation. When the black students took a vote, Thomas was the only one of the 25 to vote against the separate wing. When the school set up an all-black corridor in the dorm the following fall, Thomas moved in, but he brought John Siraco with him, along with his Malcolm X poster.

Thomas did not go home during the summers. He stayed in Worcester, working one year at a chrome-plating plant and another year at a construction site. (Ironically, he had joined a demonstration at the site the year before, protesting the building of a large development that would displace low-income residents.) He rarely went to parties during his free time, and he was usually shy around women. But in February 1969, he met Kathy Ambush, a local college student, at a campus cafeteria during a weekend in which the all-male Holy Cross was testing the waters of going coed. Thomas and Ambush began dating, and on June 5, 1971, the day after his graduation, they were married at All Saints Episcopal Church in Worcester.

During his senior year at Holy Cross, Thomas felt the desire to "go out and change the world overnight," an attitude shared by many educated young people. Determined to go back to Savannah and right the wrongs he had grown up with, he decided to go to law school. Later, he told a Senate confirmation hearing, "The reason I became a lawyer was to make sure that minorities, individuals who did not have access to this society, gained access. . . . I may differ with others on how best to do that, but the objective has always been to include those who have been excluded."

Returning to Holy Cross after graduation, Thomas counsels a student. During his college years, he had always urged other black students to be open-minded and to resist the impulse to cut themselves off from the white majority.

At the time of Thomas's graduation, Yale University Law School had recently begun its own affirmative action plan. In 1969, they had admitted more than 40 black students in a class of 200, but not all the students were qualified, and there were problems. The next year, Yale cut back to 20 black students in the class that included future president Bill Clinton. In the fall of 1971, Thomas was one of 12 blacks out of 165 in the first-year class.

"We were told we had been admitted on merit, but I was always ambivalent about this claim," he later said. "Were we or were we not? Even if we were there on merit, we knew we were also there as blacks, and it was clear to me that we were perceived as being there based on race. You had to prove yourself every day because the presumption was that you were dumb and didn't deserve to be there."

He did not want to be accepted anywhere as some form of compensation for injustices done to past generations. He felt that he had the credentials and ability to be at Yale, regardless of special treatment.

"This thing about how they let me into Yale—that kind of stuff offends me," he told Juan Williams in the *Atlantic Monthly* in 1987. "All they did was stop stopping us."

Money was a constant problem for Clarence and Kathy Thomas. Clarence applied for scholarships, but the only help he received was a pair of $250 checks from the Eastern Star in Savannah, a Masonic organization his mother belonged to. During his first summer in New Haven, he worked at a legal aid center. From time to time he felt despondent. Seeking encouragement, he subscribed to *Success* magazine and began to clip out snippets of wisdom —"keys

In the fall of 1971, Thomas entered Yale Law School as part of an affirmative action program. He later opposed such programs, arguing that black students could not enjoy a genuine sense of achievement if they were given preference because of their skin color.

to success"—which he stuffed into his wallet. Soon he was carrying more clippings than cash. One quote that stayed with him came from Bobby Knight, the legendary basketball coach at Indiana University: "The question isn't whether you have the will to win; the question is whether you have the will to prepare." Years later, this aphorism drove him to get up at 4:00 A.M. day after day to train for the Marine Marathon, held every October in Washington, D.C.

When asked to lead a campaign to get more black students admitted to the law school, Thomas refused. He was well aware that the dropout rate among blacks was high, as it had been at Holy Cross. Those who succeeded often came from middle-class families and were least in need of preferential treatment. "Look at what's happening to the masses," he said. "Those are my people. They are just where they were before any of these policies." He preferred that any affirmative action be based on financial need rather than race alone.

Black law students were expected to concentrate on civil rights law, but Thomas took only one civil rights course. He concentrated instead on traditional business, tax, and property law. His confidence rose as he competed successfully with white students in analyzing intricate legal problems. He did not back away from challenges. Once he got a poor grade in a course taught by one of the toughest teachers in the school. Instead of avoiding that teacher, he signed up for another course with him. He then deliberately chose to write his senior essay for the same teacher, earning an honors grade.

On February 15, 1973, a son, Jamal Adeen, was born to Clarence and Kathy Thomas in New Haven. The family spent the next summer in Savannah, where Clarence worked for a law firm.

Every spring, recruiters from large law firms buzzed around the nation's major law schools, hoping

John C. Danforth, photographed in 1976 during his successful campaign for the U.S. Senate. As attorney general of the state of Missouri, Danforth gave Thomas his first job as a lawyer.

to hire top students. When they interviewed Thomas, they saw black skin first, lawyer second. They emphasized that he would be given time off to do free legal work for the poor but made no mention of that to white prospects. Thomas kept looking, intent on finding someone who would ignore his race.

He later explained, "The perception was that you were never accepted as qualified, even if you were in fact overqualified. Prospective employers dismissed our grades and diplomas, assuming we got both primarily because of preferential treatment. No matter how well we had done on exams, our grades were suspect."

Wishing to return to Georgia, he interviewed with several large firms in Atlanta. But he felt demeaned by the questions they asked—"about things I had done in the eighth grade more than law school"—which he felt were reserved for black applicants only. If the purpose of the interviewers was to make him feel uncomfortable and unwanted, they succeeded. "I was adamant that I was not going to play that game," Thomas recalled.

Still seeking a color-blind employer, he noticed a small card tacked on the Yale bulletin board inviting applicants to work for John C. Danforth, the attorney general of the state of Missouri. A friend encouraged him to apply and arranged for him to meet Danforth when the young official was in New Haven. Danforth promised to treat Thomas the same as everyone else in his office and to work him harder for less money than any other job in America. "But there is plenty of room at the top," Danforth promised.

Skeptical but intrigued by Danforth's candor and optimism, Thomas took the job. Along with Kathy and Jamal, he prepared to go west to Jefferson City, Missouri, where he would find everything that Danforth had promised him.

6

THE POLITICS OF TURMOIL
·❦·

I N THE SUMMER of 1974, Thomas was studying for the Missouri bar exam in St. Louis, Missouri. There he met another aspiring attorney, Cliff Faddis, and the two became close friends. Both had jobs waiting in Jefferson City, where they later played pickup basketball together and watched football on Thomas's color TV. "We spent a lot of time with other guys in the attorney general's office," said Faddis, who worked at the Missouri Department of Revenue. "What stood out in my mind about Thomas was his integrity. We talked about changes we would like to see in the system, but he never spoke ill of it, never complained, never expressed anger. He was always positive about how hard we had to work to succeed and how we should all—black and white—learn to live together. And he never swore."

Thomas became a member of the Missouri bar on September 14, 1974, and three days later argued his first case before the Missouri Supreme Court. "It was a criminal case," he recalled. "We had a small staff and they needed somebody to argue it. Neil McFarland, another assistant [attorney general], took me upstairs to the courtroom, introduced me as a new member of the bar, and left me there alone. I thought I was going to die."

Clarence Thomas in 1982, shortly after his appointment as chairman of the Equal Opportunity Employment Commission (EEOC). After Thomas came to Washington, D.C., as a legislative assistant to Senator Danforth in 1978, his career was rapidly advanced by the Republican party leadership.

True to his word, John Danforth worked Thomas hard, paid him little ($11,000), and treated him the same as everybody else. Thomas worked on tax, corporate, and criminal cases. In 1976, after Danforth was elected to the United States Senate, Thomas went to work for the Monsanto Chemical Company at a salary of $20,000. Two and a half years later, Danforth asked him to come to Washington as a legislative assistant.

To Thomas, Washington, D.C., represented a forum where lively debates and candid exchanges of views on important issues took place. He soon discovered that this was not always true. His opinions on affirmative action and quotas and his emphasis on the duties and responsibilities of blacks to make the most of their new opportunities without relying on government help placed him at odds with the recog-

Still an avid athlete, Thomas puts a move on his old friend and fellow attorney Cliff Faddis during a pickup basketball game in Washington, D.C.

nized civil rights leaders and black politicians. He found himself shunned and labeled a traitor to his race for not "thinking black." He was also called insensitive and a dupe of white conservatives. This animosity surprised and disappointed him, but it did not deter him. "I decided to be my own person and seek my own path," he later said.

Thomas continued to advocate that society simply "stop stopping us" and allow blacks to earn their way into the economic mainstream through self-help and individual effort. He quoted with approval the 19th-century antislavery activist Frederick Douglass, who wrote, "All that any man has a right to expect, ask, give or receive in this world is fair play."

At a 1980 meeting of black conservatives in San Francisco, Thomas expressed his opinions in a speech that brought him to the attention of people working for the newly elected Republican president, Ronald Reagan. In the spring of 1981, the Reagan administration nominated him to be assistant secretary for civil rights in the Department of Education, and he faced his first Senate confirmation hearing.

Initially, Thomas resisted being placed in the seemingly "black" job of enforcing civil rights laws in schools and universities. He wanted to prove that a black official could perform equally well in other roles. But education was important to him, and he was concerned that efforts to integrate white colleges might drain state money from the traditional black colleges, such as Savannah State. "We don't get smarter just because we sit next to white people in class," he later told a reporter.

He had served at the Department of Education less than a year when the Reagan administration had another job for him. The Equal Employment Opportunity Commission (EEOC) needed a new chairman. When Reagan's first choice backed out in the face of strong opposition, Reagan nominated Thomas, who was approved by the Senate with only two dissenting votes after routine hearings.

The EEOC's purpose was to enforce federal laws that forbade employers to discriminate on the basis of color, gender, or religion when hiring and promoting people. When Clarence Thomas became EEOC chairman on May 17, 1982, the agency was in disarray. He found no paper, no pencils, not even a chair in the chairman's office. A beleaguered outfit with a $140 million budget, the agency had had seven different chairmen in its 17-year existence. Morale among the 3,000 employees was as low as could be. Almost every budget request for the EEOC was routinely slashed by the Democratic Congress. The Republicans—who opposed government regulation of business—had always hated the agency, and the Democrats hated the Republicans who were now in charge of it. Employers had the impression that the government was not really interested in enforcing the laws against discrimination, so they often ignored them.

Thomas turned the agency around, stressing professional standards, dedication to EEOC objectives, and sensitivity and support for all employees, regardless of their positions or status. When Vice-Chairman Ricky Silberman first joined the commission, she asked Thomas how he wished her to vote on a matter she was not familiar with. Based on her experience with other government commissions, she expected him to try to influence her vote. "Abstain on every vote until you know what you're doing," Thomas told her. "Then vote the way you think is right."

One of the first cases he settled was a $42.5 million agreement with General Motors that covered numerous claims and was the largest settlement in EEOC history. More than $10 million of the money went to black colleges; engineering and technology scholarships were set up; women's groups and His-

panic, Native American, and Asian institutions also benefited.

Thomas's main objective was fairness for people who faced bias on the job, not collective preferences. He fought vigorously to correct individual acts of discrimination rather than try to undo everything that was ever done in the past. His attitude of looking ahead, seeking to insure fairness in the future, was nothing new for him. He remembered that as a teenager he had often played blackjack for pennies on the back porch. "Somebody was always marking the cards," he recalled. One day, Thomas accused a boy of cheating. A fight broke out. In the confusion, everybody grabbed for the pennies in the pot, which went to the quick and the strong, not to those who had been cheated. There was no way to divvy up the money fairly to compensate the losers, so Thomas

Flanked by two General Motors executives, Thomas signs a landmark agreement with the giant automaker in October 1983. Sued by the EEOC for discrimination in the workplace, General Motors contributed $42.5 million to a variety of causes benefiting minorities.

suggested they resume playing with a new deck of cards and a promise of no more cheating.

Starting anew with a guarantee of a level playing field for all was at the heart of his view of what government should do.

"America was founded on the philosophy of individual rights, not group rights," he has said. "I believe in compensation for actual victims, not for people whose only claim to victimization is that they are members of an historically oppressed group." He questioned some black leaders' emphasis on rights over the practical goal of preparing people for employment. "It's like protecting my right to be a concert pianist when I cannot play the piano," he explained.

From the start, Thomas drew fire from all sides because he did not believe in quotas, affirmative action, or the kind of broad, sweeping class-action lawsuits that most Democrats and black organizations preferred, but which rarely produced real benefits. In fact, under Thomas the EEOC instituted more class-action suits than ever before, but the suits were brought on behalf of specific groups of employees who had suffered real discrimination.

Despite the agency's successes, Thomas's agenda so infuriated black congressmen that they would not even meet with him to discuss matters affecting the agency. "We tried desperately to meet with all of them," Thomas said. "In January 1985, Representative Mickey Leland, the head of the Congressional Black Caucus, met with me for lunch one day and that was it." Later on, the newly elected black congressman John Lewis agreed to see Thomas when the EEOC was trying to obtain better offices. "He was the first," Thomas recalled, "to help me run the agency or help the agency itself."

Black politicians and spokesmen were angered by Thomas's opposition to affirmative action. "You were helped by it," they told him. "You wouldn't be where you are if not for it." Thomas realized that he was in a no-win situation on this issue; even those who favored preferential treatment often resented the people who received it. Many black Americans believed that minorities benefited from preferences. But Thomas felt that affirmative action was, at best, a mixed blessing, resulting in the denigration of the legitimate achievements of blacks.

Thomas also made it clear that he had no use for quotas; the Civil Rights Act of 1964 made no mention of them as a remedy for past discrimination. "I have problems with any system that says if we're going to hire you, we're going to give you an advantage specifically because you are one color or another," he once said. "That kind of system worked against minorities in the past."

Thomas rejected the idea that employers had to keep their workforce 30 percent black just because the community's population was 30 percent black; he pointed out that if quotas were to be the rule, the government could charge some colleges with discrimination against whites because their basketball teams were all black.

By challenging the agendas of the established civil rights organizations, Thomas sparked accusations that he had forgotten who he was and where he came from. But over and over, he heard his grandfather's words: "What's good for the gander is good for the goose—one set of rules for everybody." As he grew older, he found himself agreeing more and more with Myers Anderson's beliefs.

In the midst of Thomas's first two tumultuous years at the EEOC, a series of unsettling events made him think of quitting. The first occurred promptly at noon on March 30, 1983, when Myers Anderson sat down at his kitchen table in Savannah for lunch. He collapsed and was taken to St. Joseph Hospital, where he died. At the funeral, Thomas cried like a baby for the first time in his adult life. A month later, on May 1, Tina Anderson also passed away.

In 1984, after 13 years of marriage, Clarence and Kathy Thomas divorced. They had been separated for three years, and they parted as friends. Thomas requested custody of Jamal, and Kathy agreed. Caring for Jamal, as his grandfather had cared for him, was important to Thomas. Even though he struggled with the role of being a single parent raising an adolescent son, he still managed to set firm, high standards of behavior for Jamal.

The pressure of his job at the EEOC was more than Thomas had bargained for, and combined with the upheavals in his personal life, it was almost too

The great abolitionist Frederick Douglass (1817–95) had a profound influence on Thomas's political ideas. As EEOC chairman, Thomas sought to follow Douglass by advocating self-help by blacks as an alternative to sweeping government action.

much for him to handle. He thought of looking for a less stressful job, but ultimately Thomas was the product of his grandfather, who had always refused to give in. He never forgot it nor let anyone else forget. It seemed to his EEOC colleagues that he could not get through a meeting without mentioning his grandfather at least once. "When the civil rights people indict me," he once said, "the man they are indicting is him. Let them call him from the grave and indict him."

Thomas believed that the black leaders who opposed him wanted all blacks to speak with one voice—theirs. But Thomas had invested too much in becoming his own man to let himself be swallowed up into a faceless mass. "Is it really more laudable to make a man afraid to express his beliefs than it is to make him ashamed of the color of his skin?" he asked a Law Day gathering at Mercer University on May 1, 1993. "Does it make sense to criticize someone who says all blacks look alike, then praise those who insist that all blacks think alike?"

Thomas resisted putting people into categories. He felt equally at ease among professors or janitors, blacks or whites. He had many white friends, but he did not cater to their prejudices or insecurities. If any of them ever seemed uneasy in his presence, that was their problem; he saw no need to expend energy trying to make them more comfortable. He also taught some of his white friends what it was like to be black in Washington "The world wasn't like they perceived it to be," he recalled. "We'd be walking along and I would ask them to hail a cab for me and when one stopped I'd hop in. The drivers, even the black ones, would holler and curse at them because I got in instead of the white guy."

If Thomas was a captive of the white Republican conservatives, as some of his attackers described him, he showed no signs of it. As much as he defended the record of the Reagan administration, he chastised the Republicans for their blatant indifference to black voters. Ultimately, he felt as much an outsider within the administration as among black leaders. "It appeared often that our white counterparts actually hid from our advice," he said. "There was a general sense that we were being avoided and circumvented."

Despite the harpooning he was taking from all directions, Thomas was nominated for a second term in 1986. His friend Senator Danforth asked him why he wanted to continue in the position, which was not seen by Washington insiders as an effective springboard to higher office. "I have unfinished work that I have to do," Thomas replied.

At a civil rights forum in New York in May 1986, Thomas met Virginia Lamp, a labor relations attorney. Lamp, a native of Omaha, Nebraska, had always been interested in politics and dreamed of running for Congress. Thomas felt happy and comfortable in her company; they shared similar views on many subjects. A year later, on May 30, 1987, they were married in a Methodist church in Omaha. They bought a home in a new development in Alexandria, Virginia, just outside Washington and lived a quiet suburban life that included lawn mowing, car washing, and neighborhood barbecues.

The dictates of ambition might have caused Thomas to soften his opinions or at least be less outspoken in order to defuse the hostility of his critics. But that would not have been Clarence Thomas. He never hesitated to take a poke at the politics of race. In a commencement speech at Savannah State College on June 9, 1985, he told the graduates, "I had the benefit of people who knew they had to walk a straighter line, climb a taller mountain and carry a heavier load. They took all that segregation and prejudice would allow them and at the same time fought to remove those awful barriers. . . . You all have a much tougher road to travel. Not only do you have to contend with the ever-present bigotry, you must do so with a recent tradition that almost requires you to wallow in excuses. You now have a popular national rhetoric which says that you can't learn because of racism, you can't raise babies you make because of racism, you can't get up in the mornings because of racism. Unlike me, you must not only overcome the repressiveness of racism, you must also overcome the lure of excuses. You have twice the job I had. . . . Do not be lured by sirens and purveyors of misery who profit from constantly regurgitating all that is wrong with black Americans and blaming these problems on others."

Thomas refused to knock the political system and celebrated it even when other black leaders did not. When Supreme Court justice Thurgood Marshall refrained from celebrating the 200th anniversary of the Constitution in 1988, he explained that he was doing so because the original Constitution had not abolished slavery. (Slavery was abolished by the Thirteenth Amendment to the Constitution, adopted in 1865.) Thomas said, "I have felt the pain of racism as much as anyone else. Yet I am wild about the Constitution and the Declaration of Independence. . . . I believe in the American . . . dream because I've seen it in my own life."

By 1989, Thomas had grown tired of both public life and Washington. He had spent his thirties as a magnet for controversy, and he felt it was time to pursue something more satisfying and rewarding. Managing the EEOC had given him valuable experience in running what amounted to a big business. Like many high government officials before him, he thought this experience would transfer to the business world, where he could earn enough money to buy the black Corvette he wanted to replace his beat-up 1973 Chevy.

Thomas addresses graduates of Savannah State College after receiving an honorary degree in 1990. Shortly afterward, he left his post at the EEOC to become a federal judge.

But George Bush, who had succeeded Ronald Reagan as president in 1989, had other ideas. One day, Thomas received a call from someone in the Justice Department, asking him to attend a breakfast meeting. At the meeting, he was asked if he would accept the nomination to be a judge on the U.S. Court of Appeals for the District of Columbia.

"I wasn't interested in being a judge," Thomas recalled. "I wanted to get out of public life and out of Washington. I didn't see it as a job for a guy who is 40 years old. I had never had any interest in it, which is the irony of ironies." Ricky Silberman, Thomas's second-in-command at the EEOC, urged her boss to take the judgeship. "I thought it would be the perfect place for Thomas, who is at heart an intellectual who loves thinking through ideas and getting to the heart of a matter," she said. "But he was reluctant."

Finally, Thomas was persuaded by the arguments of Silberman and other friends. On July 11, President Bush announced the nomination, and Thomas faced his fourth confirmation hearing. There was one consolation: being a judge would take him out of the politics of turmoil.

EEOC staff members were sorry to see him leave. Many took personal time off to attend the hearings and lend their support. In recognition of Thomas's service at the agency and his success in securing better office facilities for them, they petitioned to have their headquarters named for him. (There is now a bronze plaque in the lobby, announcing that the building has been dedicated to Thomas.)

During the hearings, which took place in February 1990, Thomas conceded that his opinions were unusual for a black official. His views had put him in a difficult and uncomfortable position, being spurned by other black political figures. But, he said, "It's a choice between principle and popularity." A March 15 editorial in the *Washington Post* said, "[Thomas's] experiences should contribute to making him a good judge." In July, he was approved by the Senate, 98–2.

Unknown to Thomas, the Bush administration had a long-term goal: Thomas's appointment to the Court of Appeals would be a stepping-stone to the Supreme Court once a vacancy occurred.

"That was their plan," Silberman insisted. "But it was not Clarence Thomas's." ❧

7

"A HIGH-TECH LYNCHING"

Intense and thoughtful, Thomas listens to opening remarks as the Senate Judiciary Committee considers his nomination to the Supreme Court. The confirmation hearings, which began on September 10, 1991, developed into a riveting drama that engrossed the entire nation.

THE JULY 1, 1991, announcement of Clarence Thomas's nomination for associate justice of the Supreme Court touched off a massive inquiry into his past. Agents of the Federal Bureau of Investigation (FBI) launched a routine background check, as they do in the case of every nominee to a high position. This time they were vastly outnumbered by television, newspaper, and magazine reporters, who swarmed into Pin Point and Savannah, looking for the people and places in Thomas's life. (One writer, unable to locate Pin Point on a map of Georgia, accused Thomas of inventing it to romanticize his childhood.) Reporters broke into the garage of his Virginia home and went through his garbage cans, seeking clues to what he ate, what kind of cigars he smoked, what he read, even what he jotted down or doodled on scraps of paper. As Senator Alan Simpson of Wyoming commented, "They've culled this guy's record better than grain drills in a pasture."

Just as Leola Williams had feared when she saw her son standing beside the president on television, the phones at her home and the hospital never stopped ringing. "There were cameramen everywhere," she said. "For a while they got after one lady at the hospital who looked like me, taking her picture, and she was taking all the attention."

To prepare Thomas for the confimation hearings, President Bush assigned a team of coaches to work with him. For two months, they met with Thomas for hours at a time. They formed a "murder board" that peppered him with all the hostile questions he might be asked. Thomas's handlers advised him how to act, what to say, and how to avoid controversy during the weeks leading up to the September hearings. They studied the legal cases and issues he might be asked about, knowing that everything he had ever said or written on such hot topics as abortion, natural law, rights of privacy, and affirmative action would be fair game for inspection. Senator Danforth, whose high reputation among other senators and willingness to actively support Thomas were key factors in Bush's choice, took part in the practice sessions.

One ritual of the process involved making the rounds of senators' offices to let them get acquainted with the nominee informally. Most nominees limited themselves to 10 or so such visits with key senators; Thomas called on a record 59 of the 100 senators. But he felt uncomfortable being muzzled by his handlers; he was not used to subduing his opinions and sticking to small talk.

He was also aware of the hostility he faced. "When you're up against those confirmation hearings, it's like going through Dante's Inferno," he told a writer. "When you get up there you just hope you don't get destroyed so that even if you don't make it you can go on with your life."

The attacks on Thomas began long before the hearings. His opponents combed through millions of documents searching for what some people have called "crazy quotes," phrases of three or four words that might be pulled out and used to embarrass, confuse, or intimidate him.

The central question facing blacks was how a black man could oppose policies that were said to help black people. But Thomas believed that those policies had failed and would continue to fail, and he cited the evidence he saw around him of the lack of progress of most blacks. Leaders of the NAACP were in a dilemma. They were always eager to see blacks reach high positions, but this one had publicly criticized them. "I don't see how we can support someone who stands against everything we stand for," said one board member. Ultimately, the NAACP board did not support him, voting 50–1 to fight his confirmation.

The Congressional Black Caucus also voted to reject Thomas, with only one person, Representative Gary Franks, dissenting. The Leadership Conference on Civil Rights, a coalition of 85 groups representing women, minorities, labor, and the disabled came out against Thomas, as did the National Baptist Convention, the nation's largest black church group. In all, about 120 organizations took a position on the Thomas nomination. It was open season, and the shots came from all directions.

The opponents' rhetoric was sometimes heated and personal. Derrick Bell, a black law professor at Harvard, wrote, "The choice of a black like Clarence Thomas replicates the slavemasters' practice of elevating to overseer . . . those slaves willing to mimic the masters' views." USA Today columnist Barbara Reynolds charged, "If he can't paint himself white he is going to think white and marry a white woman." Another critic compared Thomas unfavorably to the great abolitionist Frederick Douglass, ignoring the parallel between Thomas's ideas and Douglass's belief that blacks should strive to educate themselves and to help one another rather than depend on the government.

To those supporting Thomas, the nominee's willingness to say what he thought was his greatest strength. John Danforth called him "a person who is not a stereotype of anything. He's an independent person who thinks for himself. If people have a preconceived notion of what a black lawyer should be, that's not fair." At a conference of black public officials, Gwendolyn King, then commissioner of Social Security, said, "There is not and should not be a correct way of African-American thinking. We are as entitled to diversity of thought, opinion, and perspective as any other segment of society. When someone else tries to deny us that diversity, it is a crime. When we deny it to ourselves, that . . . is a tragedy."

There were some people, such as Guido Calabresi, dean of Yale Law School, who disagreed with Thomas's thinking but still supported his nomination. "Unlike many on the court," Calabresi noted, "he does know the deep need of the poor and especially of poor blacks and wants to help. . . . How can [the other justices] know what discrimination really means?"

Many of the people Thomas had worked with at the EEOC took time off to support his nomination. Judges he served with on the Court of Appeals spoke up for him. Longtime friends, questioned by dozens of reporters, testified to his integrity, intellectual ability, and compassion. Frank Washington, a law school classmate, said, "You are talking about a person who understands what it is like to be black and poor in this country, and to face the worst kinds of prejudice. . . . He will not block those [experiences] from his thinking."

On August 1, Thomas enjoyed a brief respite from the daily shelling. An organization supporting him

brought 45 of his relatives and friends from Georgia to Washington to lobby senators on his behalf. They met for breakfast with Thomas, who enjoyed the touch of home. The delegation's feelings were summed up by one member who said, "All I can say to his critics is they don't know the man, 'cause Clarence Thomas will never forget."

Finally, on the morning of September 10, 1991, Clarence Thomas sat alone, without handlers or aides beside him, at a long table covered with a thick green cloth, facing the 14 white men who made up the Senate Judiciary Committee. Behind him sat his wife, his son, Jamal, now 18, his mother, and his sister. (Myers Thomas, a successful accountant, had professional commitments and could not attend the hearings.) The space between Thomas and his interrogators was crisscrossed by heavy cables that would carry every word to radio and television audiences around the world. Thomas would have to choose his words with care. He knew that everything he said, every gesture he made, every expression that passed across his face, would be magnified. The smallest details would be examined, analyzed, and commented on by friends, opponents, and millions of curious, uncommitted citizens.

The Senate Caucus Room, with its 35-foot ceilings and huge crystal chandeliers, was jammed be-

Admittedly nervous, Thomas faces the Judiciary Committee in the Senate Caucus Room. "When you get up there you just hope you don't get destroyed," he said, "so that even if you don't make it you can go on with your life."

yond its seating capacity of 300. The crowd included Sister Mary Virgilius Reidy, Thomas's eigth-grade teacher, who would testify in his behalf, and Rosa Parks, whose refusal to move from her seat on a bus in Montgomery, Alabama, had led to Martin Luther King, Jr's. entry into the civil rights movement.

Dressed in a dark suit and red tie, the 43-year-old Thomas sat nervously adjusting his glasses, then folding his arms in front of him. Senator Joseph Biden, the committee chairman, administered the oath: "Judge Thomas, do you solemnly swear to tell the truth, the whole truth, and nothing but the truth, so help you God?" Thomas answered, "I do."

Biden, while outlining the procedures to be followed, commented on how young Thomas was for a prospective Supreme Court justice. "I've aged in the last 10 weeks," Thomas replied.

Thomas listened as each of the 14 senators made his own opening comments. Some praised him; others expressed their concerns about his views and indicated the areas they intended to question him about. It was 3:00 P.M. before Thomas's turn came. He took

Thomas's mother, Leola Williams, and his sister, Emma Mae Martin, show the strain of witnessing Thomas's grilling by the Judiciary Committee. "If I wasn't a Christian, I'd take my Bible and slap that senator in the head," Emma Mae remarked at one point.

less than 15 minutes to talk about who he was and where he came from, describing his childhood in Pin Point and the influence his grandparents and the nuns had had on him.

Throughout Tuesday, Wednesday, Thursday, Friday, and the following Monday, Thomas was grilled and badgered. Coached to avoid commenting on any subject that might come up in a future case before the Court, Thomas exasperated his opponents by seeming to disavow opinions he had expressed over the years and refusing to be drawn into discussions of a number of topics. In some exchanges, the level of animosity got so high that Thomas's sister, Emma Mae, was heard to mutter, "If I wasn't a Christian I'd take my Bible and slap that senator in the head."

Nowhere were the proceedings followed more intently than in Savannah and Pin Point. Friends and relatives Thomas had grown up with, teachers and schoolmates, elders who had disciplined him in the dusty yards of Pin Point and on the streets of Savannah all rooted for him and prayed for him. The hearing dominated the local newspapers. "It makes me sick the way they're treating him," said a cousin, Viola Martin. "I don't like their tone." "He's been dragged in the mud and slung around," said another relative. "To see him handle it so well is wonderful. He's still holding his head up. If it was me, I'd be down their throats."

Thomas's sense of humor occasionally eased the unending tension. When asked what his minor had been at Holy Cross, he said, "I think protests."

The night before the hearings began, he had probably been the only person in Washington rooting for the Dallas Cowboys as they lost to the Washington Redskins on ABC's "Monday Night Football." At one point he commented, "I am totally convinced that every referee in those games is a Redskins fan, but none would admit it."

Thomas has a joyous reunion with Sister Mary Virgilius Reidy, his eighth-grade teacher, during the confirmation hearings. Sister Mary Virgilius joined a large delegation of friends and relatives who traveled to Washington, D.C., in order to express their support for Thomas.

On Monday, September 16, the direct questioning ended, and a smiling, relieved Thomas kissed his wife and briskly left the ornate Caucus Room, where a parade of 90 witnesses would subsequently speak for or against him. When the hearings concluded four days later, Thomas was confident that he had the votes to win approval in the Senate, although he expected the Judiciary Committee to be evenly divided—they fulfilled his prediction, with seven voting for and seven voting against him. Under Senate rules, the deadlock sent the nomination to the Senate floor.

Unknown to Thomas, during the week he had been testifying a woman had secretly contacted the committee with allegations against him of improper conduct toward her when she had worked for him at the EEOC.

Early on the afternoon of September 25, Cliff Faddis arrived at Washington National Airport to visit Thomas and help him celebrate the expected victory. "Whenever I came to town he would pick me up at the airport," Faddis recalled. "This time when I called, he said, 'Butch, something's come up. Take a cab.' I knew then that something was wrong."

Faddis had landed just as two FBI agents were informing Thomas that a woman named Anita Hill had charged him with sexual harassment in a number of incidents dating back eight or nine years. Hill, a black attorney, had worked for Thomas at the Department of Education and had gone with him to the EEOC. She had left to take a teaching position, which she had gotten partly on the strength of a letter of recommendation Thomas had written for her. They had remained friends, and Hill had called him for help from time to time. She was now a professor at the University of Oklahoma Law School.

Hill had never intended to make her charges public; she had been assured by people working to defeat Thomas that once he was confronted with her accusations, he would withdraw his name rather than face the allegations publicly. But that did not happen. Hearing Hill named as his accuser, Thomas said incredulously, "Anita? You've got to be kidding. This can't be true."

When Faddis arrived at the house, Thomas told him what had happened. "Butch," Thomas said, "I'm lower than a hog's belly."

"Would you believe that a friend would do this?" Thomas asked over and over. "I have to defend myself against something that never happened." "He felt betrayed by a friend he had tried to help," Faddis said later.

Ricky Silberman reacted to the news with disbelief. "When they called me and said a sexual harassment charge had been made against Clarence Thomas, I laughed. . . . It was preposterous on its face. Thomas had put Hill's name on the list of people he

wanted to testify for him. . . . Would he have
listed her to speak for him if there had been anything
that smacked of sexual harassment?"

When Thomas did not withdraw, Hill reluctantly
agreed to tell her story to the Judiciary Committee.
But the hearings had ended, and the FBI had found
no independent evidence to back up Hill's charges.
For the next few days, a battle raged behind closed
doors; some committee members wanted to reopen
the hearings, perhaps in a closed session, while others
saw no reason for any further hearings, private or
public.

The public remained unaware of the controversy
until Sunday, October 6, two days before the Senate
was scheduled to vote on the Thomas confirmation.
At that point, National Public Radio and a New York
newspaper broke the story. Pressure from a variety of
organizations and the media forced a furious daylong
debate in the Senate.

Thomas and his wife spent Tuesday, October 8,
at the home of friends while the 100 senators quar-
reled about reopening the hearings. Senator Danforth
called and reminded him that the hearings could only
be reopened if all 100 senators agreed. Danforth
himself could stop the hearings from reopening and
prevent Anita Hill from testifying. He also pointed
out that the charges had eroded Thomas's support in
the Senate; if Danforth were to force the confirmation vote that day, Thomas's nomination might be
rejected. He left the decision up to Thomas, who told
Danforth to put off the vote and let the hearings
resume. "They have taken from me what I worked 43
years to create—my reputation," Thomas declared. "I
want to clear my name."

Many of Thomas's old friends called to offer their
help. "I've never felt this bad in my whole life,"
Thomas told Lester Johnson. "I've been through days
when they called me nigger, told me I was thick-

Anita Hill smiles in response to a question during her testimony before the Senate Judiciary Committee. Hill, a professor of law at the University of Oklahoma, alleged that Thomas had made suggestive remarks to her when she was an attorney at the EEOC.

lipped and had nappy hair, but this affects my whole family. . . . If they're going to attack my philosophy, fine. If they're going to attack me for being an Uncle Tom, that's okay. But if they're going to attack me for sexual harassment, that's the bottom. The only thing that's keeping me up is God."

On the morning of Friday, October 11, Thomas returned to the all-too-familiar Senate Caucus Room he thought he had put behind him. Every TV network broadcast the hearings live. Throughout the country, millions of people interrupted their usual routine to watch the drama unfold over the next three days.

Clarence Thomas, free of handlers and advisers, was angry, and Danforth urged him to express his feelings. With his wife and Danforth sitting behind him, Thomas began by apologizing for anything he might ever have said or done that Anita Hill might have taken as offensive, though he could think of nothing.

"But," he went on in a booming voice, "enough is enough. I am not going to allow myself to be further humiliated in order to be confirmed. . . . No job is worth what I have been through."

The nationwide audience was poised for a bombshell. Thomas sounded as if he was about to withdraw. But his foes' hopes were quickly dashed. "Confirm me if you want. Don't confirm me if you are so led. But let this process end. Let me and my family regain our lives. I never asked to be nominated. It was an honor. Little did I know the price, but it is too high. . . . My name has been harmed. My friends have been harmed. There is nothing this committee, this body, or this country can do to give me back my good name. Nothing."

In Savannah, Thomas's mother, Leola Williams, became ill. She could not work or eat, and in a short time she lost 25 pounds. "I couldn't stand to see them dirtying Clarence's name the way they were," she said. On Sunday morning she arose from her sickbed and went to Pin Point to pray for Clarence at the Sweet Fields of Eden Baptist Church.

When Anita Hill was called to testify, she repeated the suggestive remarks she claimed Thomas had made to her and spoke of the pornographic films he had described to her. She spoke calmly, confidently, and convincingly. Under harsh questioning, she stuck to her story.

Thomas returned to the table and heatedly denied every accusation made by Hill. "This is a circus," he said. "It's a national disgrace. And from my standpoint as a black American, as far as I'm concerned, it is a high-tech lynching for uppity blacks who in any way deign to think for themselves, to do for themselves, to have different ideas, and it is a message that unless you kowtow to the old order, this is what will happen to you. You will be lynched, destroyed, caricatured by a committee of the United States Senate rather than hung from a tree."

Reactions to Thomas's reference to a lynching came swiftly and, like everything else in the battle over his nomination, the opinions were sharply divided. Some people were repelled by what they called Thomas's use of the "race card," his pointed reference to his skin color and to racial prejudice, after he had pleaded for a color-blind judgment on his qualifications.

A grim-looking Thomas confers with his wife, Virginia, while responding to Anita Hill's charges of sexual harassment. "I would have preferred an assassin's bullet to this kind of living hell," he remarked.

Facing the media outside their Alexandria, Virginia, home on October 16, 1991, the Thomases express their relief and satisfaction over the Senate's 52–48 vote approving the Thomas nomination.

But those close to Thomas took a different view. "I felt that he really was being lynched," Cliff Faddis said, "just like in the old days, with a rope and no justification. I was not surprised when he put it that way. That was pure Clarence Thomas. They accused him of playing the race card. But *this* was the race card. They were hanging a black guy just like in the old days."

Ricky Silberman agreed. "The American people got to see the real Clarence Thomas there for all his warts. He was angry and should have been angry, but he defended himself on the basis of his historical experience when he said it was the lynching of a black man, a wronged man. It was a terribly authentic Clarence Thomas."

The extraordinary hearings concluded late Sunday night with testimony by friends of Thomas's who had volunteered to come from all over the country to swear that they had never heard him utter an off-color or smutty comment and had seen him treat people only with dignity and respect.

Millions of people who watched the entire proceedings intently for three days did not believe Anita Hill. Millions of others did believe her. The 100 senators were as divided as the public over which of these two conflicting, impressive, and believable strangers was telling the truth.

The final segment of the hearings produced an unprecedented outpouring of calls to senators' offices, as citizens urged their senators to vote for or against Thomas. On most weekends, the calls average 24,000 a day. On the last Saturday of the hearings, 476,000 came in. On the following Monday and Tuesday, more than one million calls were received each day, three times the normal load. Fax machines ran out of paper; voice-mail systems ran out of tape.

During the first five minutes of the final confirmation debate on Tuesday morning, October 15,

43,000 callers tried to get through to their senators. The debate raged for seven and a half hours. Almost an entire hour was consumed by Senator Robert S. Byrd of West Virginia, who cited the Bible, John Milton, William Shakespeare, and the historians of ancient Rome to explain why he was going to vote against Thomas.

NBC-TV broadcast the entire debate. The network even set up a camera in Leola Williams's kitchen so the world could see her reactions. Clarence and Virginia Thomas remained at home. To relax, Clarence occasionally went outside and shot some baskets. It was all out of his hands now.

That evening, as senators mounted the steps of the Capitol for the close of the debate and the casting of votes, they passed dozens of chanting Thomas supporters on one side of the street and an equal number of his opponents on the other side. When the roll was called, Clarence Thomas was confirmed by a vote of 52–48. Grinning with relief, Thomas hugged his wife and his friend Cliff Faddis, while Leola Williams stood in her kitchen and raised a hymn.

Later in the evening, a few dozen close friends crowded into the Thomas home and celebrated. Exhilaration overcame exhaustion. Senator Danforth spoke briefly, quoting a verse from the book of Isaiah about the suffering servant. "Clarence Thomas," he said, "you are the suffering servant of Isaiah. You have taken the iniquities and sins of all onto your shoulders."

Thomas did not intend to be anyone's servant, even Isaiah's, but he certainly agreed that it was time to put the suffering behind him. Outside, sheltered under an umbrella in the rain, he told reporters, "This is more a time for healing, not a time for anger or animosity. . . . We have to put those things behind us and go forward." ❧

8

"LET US GO FORWARD TOGETHER"

"SINCE THAT BRIGHT sunny day in Kennebunkport, there have been many difficult days as we went through the confirmation battle," Clarence Thomas told the crowd of 1,000 guests on the South Lawn of the White House on October 18, 1991, "but on this sunny day in October at the White House there is joy in the morning."

He had just taken the federal oath administered by Associate Justice Byron White, beginning the most joyful Supreme Court swearing-in celebration ever held. Hundreds of Thomas's friends, including Sister Mary Virgilius Reidy from St. John's Seminary and Father John Brooks from Holy Cross, had come from all over the country. Cousins from Pin Point mixed with federal officials and celebrities such as Sylvester Stallone and Reggie Jackson, while TV cameras recorded the event.

In his remarks, Thomas focused on the future, looking back only to thank the people who had "stood along the road of 43 years of my life. . . . Today, now, is a time to move forward, a time to look for what is good in others, what is good in our country. It's a time to see what we have in common, what we share as human beings and citizens." He closed by

Accompanied by his wife and Supreme Court Justice Byron White, Thomas acknowledges well-wishers during his swearing-in ceremony at the White House on October 18, 1991.

quoting former British prime minister Winston Churchill: "Let us go forward together."

Thomas's official installation at the Supreme Court had been scheduled for November 1, but he requested an earlier date so he could begin receiving internal court documents and hiring his four law clerks. On October 6, Chief Justice William Rehnquist administered the judicial oath at a hurried ceremony. Taking the oath with his hand on a Bible held by his wife, Thomas became the first dark-skinned black since Reconstruction to reach a high position in the country. Every other high-ranking black official during the 20th century had been light skinned.

The first day Thomas drove to his new job in his brown 1973 Chevy, he felt like a new kid in town who was starting school a month late. The Court's fall term had already begun, and Thomas had missed 17 cases. His only thought that day was of the need to get to work; but every day thereafter, as he drove into the court's underground garage, he wondered, What am I doing here?

"Justice [Lewis F.] Powell told me there wasn't a day he came to court that he didn't say to himself, 'This is incredible,' " Thomas later reflected. "And he had been the president of the American Bar Association. It'll take years for me to begin to get a glimmer of understanding of all this. I used to read Horatio Alger stuff: poor guy makes good, guy who competes against the odds and makes it—that's all I grew up on. And then all of a sudden, to wake up one morning, and think, You were born in Pin Point and here you are the 106th Justice of the Supreme Court of the United States. . . . It's an amazing thing—too much to digest. I don't know how I got here. I do not understand it."

But Thomas also believed that everything in his past had prepared him for his destiny and that he was a symbol of the possibilities awaiting those who were sufficiently dedicated.

The Supreme Court provided Thomas with no orientation or training session—just 1,000 pages of legal documents waiting to be read. A few things about the job surprised him: "The pace was a lot faster than I expected. We review more than 7,000 requests to be heard each year. We have to read the briefs of the cases we are going to hear. The cases we hear on Monday, we have to vote on on Wednesday. Those we hear on Tuesday and Wednesday, we have to vote on on Friday. So you can't say, 'Oh, well, I'll get around to reading this later.' At the same time, you are either writing opinions or reviewing opinions written by the other eight justices. The work is more analysis of the law than philosophical; there is little time to sit and think about things on the job." The basic function of the Supreme Court is to determine if state and federal laws and decisions by lower courts are consistent with the Constitution. The justices do not judge the facts of a case but decide only if the essential legal principles have been applied correctly.

Thomas described the job as one of figuring out "what the law says, not what I want it to say. There is a difference between the role of a judge and that of a policy maker. . . . Judging requires a certain impartiality, which is not the same as indifference. . . . When I hear a case, I know that something is going to happen as a result of what I decide. People's lives are affected. Even a decision not to hear a case affects people's lives. [Of the 7,000 appeals received each year, only 100 to 120 are heard.] For example, we turned down former heavyweight boxing champion Mike Tyson. [Tyson, serving a prison term in Indiana, had petitioned the court to review his conviction for rape.] Sometimes a man's life depends on the outcome. It's not a responsibility I take lightly. . . . You've taken a personal oath, and you really have

The newest member of the Supreme Court, Thomas gathers with his colleagues in the Court's conference room in November 1991. At the time, the members of the Court were (from Thomas's left) Associate Justices White, Souter, Scalia, Stevens, Blackmun, Kennedy, and O'Connor, and Chief Justice Rehnquist.

to be comfortable within yourself that what you've done when you make a decision is right."

Thomas acknowledged that he lost sleep over some difficult cases. "My grandfather used to say if it's worth doing something, it's worth doing it right. Whether you're plowing or picking beans or feeding hogs or cleaning chickens, everything you do, you do your best. I don't think I should be remembered for anything more than: he did the best job he could."

"The most difficult situation," Thomas said, "is one in which your heart wants you to do something, but the Constitution or the statute in question doesn't give you the authority. It's like watching someone close to you drowning and you can't get to them. . . . Other cases may be analytically hard, like a tough geometry problem, but you can work through them. Both types take discipline, but it takes a different type of discipline not to go with how you feel, but rather with what the law says."

The Court's procedures are ruled by tradition and seniority. As the junior justice, Thomas sat at the far right end of the bench in the courtroom. He was also in charge of the Court's annual Christmas party, held in the Great Hall. In conferences, he had the duty of recording the votes on which cases the Court would hear in the future and passing the results to the officer outside the door.

There was never anyone else in the conference room when the nine justices met. They all shook hands before getting down to business, as they did prior to entering the courtroom. As the junior judge on the three-judge Court of Appeals, Thomas had always given his opinion first in conferences. Here the chief justice spoke first. Then the discussion went around the table by seniority, and the junior justice spoke last (although discussions might erupt at any time, to the consternation of the chief justice). Thomas found the procedure to his liking; by the time his turn came, he had heard what everyone else had to say. Despite being a newcomer, he was not shy about disagreeing with his colleagues, even though he admitted that at such times "you feel a bit like a brat."

Among the cases decided during Justice Thomas's first three years on the Court was *Lee v. Weissman*, in which the Court held that there could be no prayers at high school graduations. In another case, the Court ruled that race could not be a factor in choosing a jury. In general, Thomas's opinions allied him with the conservative wing of the Court, which included Chief Justice Rehnquist, Associate Justice Byron White, and Associate Justice Antonin Scalia. As a result, his early performance drew criticism from the groups that had opposed his nomination.

Thomas was sensitive to the racial issues that often influence the criminal justice system. He wanted the death penalty to be mandatory for certain crimes rather than leaving the decision to a jury; history has shown that juries tend to inflict the death penalty more readily on blacks who kill whites than the other way around.

In his first months on the Court, Thomas routinely worked 12-hour days, spending most of that time reading and writing. He took breaks in the top-floor gym, shooting baskets or pumping iron, and was able to leave the job behind and relax at the end of the day. One day he called the ailing Thurgood Marshall and asked if he could come and visit for 15 minutes. The visit lasted more than two hours, and Thomas was grateful for the chance to become better acquainted with the man he had succeeded.

For her own part, Virginia Thomas continued to pursue a career in law and politics; as of 1994, she was senior policy coordinator for the House Republican Conference. In 1992, the Thomases built a new home out in the country. They bought two black Labrador pups, which they named Winston and Clementine. When Winnie was hit by a car and killed, the Thomases bought a replacement to keep Clemmie company. They named the dog Mike, which had been Myers Anderson's nickname.

Thomas's new status did not change Leola Williams's life. She continued to work at the hospital, and gradually the reporters stopped bothering her and the telephone did not ring so often. When she called her son's offices she would say, "May I speak to Clarence?" Reminded that callers always asked for

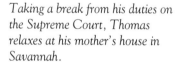
Taking a break from his duties on the Supreme Court, Thomas relaxes at his mother's house in Savannah.

"Justice Thomas," she shot back, "I didn't name him Justice Thomas. I named him Clarence. They put the Justice on there, not me."

Whenever Thomas visits his mother, Leola knows to have some of his favorite southern dishes—okra gumbo, collards, sweet potato pie—waiting for him, to get three chickens ready for frying, and not to expect any leftovers.

The part of his job Thomas enjoyed most was the opportunity to talk to students, from the youngest all the way up to college seniors. When a group of 35 fourth graders from New York City showed up at the Court in May 1992, he spent 90 minutes with them. He advised them to study two hours every day and not watch too much television. One student asked him, "How come you are on TV so much and the other justices aren't?" Thomas said he would just as soon not have all the attention.

One day another large group of elementary-school students visited the Supreme Court. Thomas spoke to them for about 15 minutes, but apparently he did not make a powerful impression on all the students. He recalled that when he invited questions, "one little guy raised his hand and stood up and asked, 'Where's Justice Thomas?' It was wonderful, so honest. . . . You get in the doldrums and you go and see those bright little faces."

Sometimes the encounters were not so enjoyable, though. "The only difficult time," Thomas remarked, "is when you have a group and there is no light in kids' eyes, no interest—no animosity or anger, just nothing, like someone had turned it off. No hope. That is bad. That makes me so despondent, I feel drained. It's important for kids to have heroes. They still want them, and to believe that if they work hard they can become something. And what do we fill them with? All these messages of despair. That's something I didn't have to live with. There was despair all around me, but there were no messages of despair."

When students asked Thomas who his own heroes were, they usually expected to hear the names of celebrities or famous people in history:

> But that's fabrication. Sure, when I was young my heroes were athletes. I am grateful to Bob Hayes for running and playing football. He was my hero. I knew he had problems. [Hayes was later jailed on drug charges.] But he didn't know there was this kid in Savannah following him. [Dallas Cowboys quarterback] Roger Staubach didn't know there was this kid watching him being a strong person, a good person, never quitting, and wanting to emulate him. I was so happy when Dan Jansen finally won an Olympic gold medal [in 1994]. That's what it's all about, perseverance and not giving up. . . . So when kids ask me who my heroes are, I say my grandfather and the people I lived among. They didn't win any awards, didn't discover anything. They lived their lives with pride and dignity. Why were they not bitter? They all had reason to be. Every one of those women worked in a kitchen. Miss Gertrude, 80 years old, still cleaned hotel rooms. But there was dignity, respect. They didn't have any money, but they set a standard. Those are the people I admire the most. They and Mrs. Cameron and the Carnegie librarians. They are my heroes. . . . One of the tragedies in our society today is that we are allowed to have so few heroes. As soon as someone is looked up to or revered, there seems to be an axiom to tear them down. My grandfather used to call that the "crabs in the basket" syndrome. Ever watch crabs in a bushel basket? They all could get out, but they don't. You can leave them without a lid on and they will all be there when you get back, because they hold onto each other with their claws, so nobody gets out.

Thomas urged high school students visiting the Court to work hard to make the most of the opportunities open to them. He advised them not to major in black studies because it would not help them get ahead in the world. He suggested instead that they major in English; it had been the hardest subject for him, but he knew that being able to express himself clearly and eloquently would be a valuable asset.

The message he carried to college students did not vary over the years: "I have been called a conservative because I feel strongly that without education, blacks don't have a prayer; because I believe values and morality have at least as much to do with babies having babies as anything else; that hard work and discipline do play a significant role in whether a person is successful or not. Based on what they try to make me believe, the manner in which they try to destroy me in the press, other blacks don't believe these things. Well, I could have sworn my grandparents and the nuns all but beat these kinds of values into me. And, applying these and similar values in my life has as much or more to do with my personal achievements as anything else."

Visitors to the white marble Supreme Court building, which contains 350 employees, are often struck by the stillness and the absence of hurry among the people inside. The justices work alone for the

Thomas talks to students taking part in a St. Louis law internship program in 1993. "It's important for kids to have heroes," he has remarked, "and to believe that if they work hard they can become something."

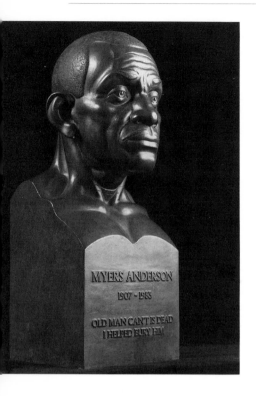

Thomas keeps this bronze bust of his grandfather Myers Anderson in his office at the Supreme Court. The bust looks down on Thomas while he labors at his desk, inspiring him to keep working hard and to be grateful for what he has achieved.

most part, consulting with their clerks, who do much of the basic digging in the law books and write summaries of their findings.

In 1994, Justice Thomas occupied a small office equipped with the Court's standard black leather sofa and chairs. Thomas usually sat at a large mahogany partner's desk, working at his word processor or reading in his high-backed chair. Between the floor-to-ceiling windows behind his desk hung a portrait of Frederick Douglass. Above the marble fireplace, there was a portait of Booker T. Washington. Small metal busts of Churchill and Horatio Alger shared space on the mantel with family photos and a framed thank-you card made by a group of children from Pittsburgh. A watercolor of the crab-packing plant in Pin Point rested on a stand-up desk in the corner.

High above Thomas's desk, a bronze bust of Myers Anderson sat alone on the top shelf of a bookcase. It was a gift from Thomas's wife. Thomas had these words inscribed on it: "Old Man Can't Is Dead—I Helped Bury Him."

"I put my grandfather up there so he would be looking down at me while I'm working," Thomas told a visitor. "Any time that I start to feel sorry for myself, I have to explain to that old man looking down on me how it is that I am in what he used to call a coat-and-tie job and I'm complaining. He went to the third grade and later had to be taught how to write his name. How could I explain to him that *I* feel put upon!

"You know what I mean?"

CHRONOLOGY

1948   Born Clarence Thomas on June 23 in Pin Point, Georgia

1955   Enrolls in St. Benedict's School in Savannah

1962   Enters St. Pius X High School

1971   Graduates from College of the Holy Cross; marries Kathy Ambush

1973   Son, Jamal Adeen is born

1974   Thomas graduates from Yale Law School; joins the staff of Missouri attorney general John C. Danforth

1976   Joins Monsanto Chemical Company

1979   Joins staff of Senator Danforth as legislative assistant

1981   Confirmed as assistant secretary for civil rights in the U.S. Department of Education

1982   Named Chairman of the Equal Employment Opportunity Commission (EEOC)

1984   Clarence and Kathy Thomas divorce

1987   Thomas marries Virginia Lamp

1989   Appointed judge of the U.S. Court of Appeals for the District of Columbia

1991   July 1: Nominated by President Bush to be an associate justice of the U.S. Supreme Court

        September 10: Confirmation hearings begin before Senate judiciary Committee

        September 27: Committee votes 7–7 on confirmation, opening the way for a vote by the full senate

        October 11: Hearings reopen to consider Anita Hill's allegations of sexual harassment

        October 15: Senate confirms Thomas by a vote of 52–48

        October 18: Thomas is sworn in as the 106th justice of the Supreme Court

FURTHER READING

Aldred, Lisa. *Thurgood Marshall*. New York: Chelsea House, 1990.

Carlson, Margaret. "Marching to a Different Drummer." *Time*, July 15, 1991.

Danforth, John C. *Resurrection: The Confirmation of Clarence Thomas*. New York: Viking, 1994.

Elshtain, Jean B. "Trial by Fury." *New Republic*, September 6, 1993.

Friedman, Leon. *The Supreme Court*. New York: Chelsea House, 1987.

Gest, Ted. "What's Ahead for Thomas." *U.S. News & World Report*, October 12, 1992.

Kaplan, David A. "Supreme Mystery." *Newsweek*, September 16, 1991.

McCaughey, Elizabeth P. "Clarence Thomas's Record as a Judge." *Presidential Studies Quarterly*, Fall 1991.

Mayer, Jane, and Jill Abramson. *Strange Justice: The Selling of Clarence Thomas*. Boston: Houghton Mifflin, 1994.

Sancton, Thomas. "Judging Thomas." *Time*, July 13, 1992.

Williams, Juan. "A Question of Fairness." *Atlantic Monthly*, February 1987.

INDEX

PICTURE CREDITS

NORMAN L. MACHT is the author of more than a dozen books for Chelsea House Publishers, including a recent biography of baseball pitcher Jim Abbott. His work also appears regularly in *Baseball Digest*, *Beckett's*, and *USA Today Baseball Weekly*. Macht is the coauthor with Dick Bartell of *Rowdy Richard*, and with Rex Barney of *Rex Barney's THANK Youuu for 50 Years in Baseball*. He is the president of Choptank Syndicate, Inc., and lives in Baltimore, Maryland.

NATHAN IRVIN HUGGINS, one of America's leading scholars in the field of black studies, helped select the titles for the BLACK AMERICANS OF ACHIEVEMENT series, for which he also served as senior consulting editor. He was the W. E. B. Du Bois Professor of History and of Afro-American Studies at Harvard University and the director of the W. E. B. Du Bois Institute for Afro-American Research at Harvard. He received his doctorate from Harvard in 1962 and returned there as a professor in 1980 after teaching at Columbia University, the University of Massachusetts, Lake Forest College, and the California State University, Long Beach. He was the author of four books and dozens of articles, including *Black Odyssey: The Afro-American Ordeal in Slavery*, *The Harlem Renaissance*, and *Slave and Citizen: The Life of Frederick Douglass*, and was associated with the Children's Television Workshop, National Public Radio, the Boston Athenaeum, the Museum of Afro-American History, the Howard Thurman Educational Trust, and Upward Bound. Professor Huggins died in 1989, at the age of 62, in Cambridge, Massachusetts.